GREEN
MARKETS

WITHDRAWN

Number 7 in the
ICEG Sector Studies Series

Since 1985 the International Center for Economic Growth, a nonprofit organization, has contributed to economic growth and human development in developing and post-socialist countries by strengthening the capacity of indigenous research institutes to provide leadership in policy debates. The Center sponsors a wide range of programs—including research, publications, conferences, seminars, and special projects advising governments—through a network of more than 250 correspondent institutes worldwide. The Center's research and publications program is organized around five series: Sector Studies; Country Studies; Studies in Human Development and Social Welfare; Occasional Papers; and Working Papers.

The Center is affiliated with the Institute for Contemporary Studies and is headquartered in Panama with the administrative office in San Francisco, California.

For further information, please contact the International Center for Economic Growth, 243 Kearny Street, San Francisco, California, 94108, USA. Phone (415) 981-5353; Fax (415) 986-4878.

ICEG Board of Overseers

GREEN
MARKETS

THE ECONOMICS OF
SUSTAINABLE DEVELOPMENT

THEODORE PANAYOTOU

Foreword by Oscar Arias

A Copublication of the International Center for Economic Growth
and the Harvard Institute for International Development

 PRESS
Institute for Contemporary Studies
San Francisco, California

© 1993 Theodore Panayotou

Publication signifies that the International Center for Economic Growth
believes a work to be a competent treatment worthy of public consideration. The findings, interpretations, and conclusions of a work are
entirely those of the author and should not be attributed to ICEG, its
affiliated organizations, its Board of Overseers, or organizations that
support ICEG.

Inquiries, book orders, and catalog requests should be addressed to ICS
Press, Institute for Contemporary Studies, 243 Kearny Street, San Francisco, California 94108 USA. Telephone: (415) 981-5353; fax: (415) 986-
4878; book orders within the continental United States: **(800) 326-0263.**

Editor: Heidi Fritschel
Indexer: Shirley Kessel
Cover designer: Ben Santora
Cover photo: Spencer Swanger/Tom Stack & Associates

Library of Congress Cataloging-in-Publication Data

Panaiotov, Todor.
    Green markets : the economics of sustainable development /
Theodore Panayotou.
        p.   cm. — (Sector studies ; no. 7)
    "A copublication of the International Center for Economic Growth
and the Harvard Institute for International Development."
    Includes bibliographical references and index.
    ISBN 1-55815-244-X.— ISBN 1-55815-222-9 (pbk.)
    1. Environmental policy—Economic aspects—Developing
countries—Case studies.   2. Sustainable development—Developing
countries—Case studies.   I. Title.   II. Series
HC59.72.P36   1993
338.9'009172'4—dc20

92-38901

To Donna, Eleni, Alexander, and Sophia,
my personal sources of sustainability

Table of Contents

Foreword

Faced with a common challenge, the human family and the environment in which it dwells share a common destiny and a common goal: survival. Never before has there been such a pressing need for a global alliance.

The partnership that will characterize mankind from now on is based upon the realization that everything is interconnected and interdependent. Today, the inhabitants of Tokyo, Amsterdam, and Denver know that their future and the future of their descendants will be profoundly marked by what Brazilian farmers do to satisfy the most basic needs of their families. Similarly, Chilean farmers have begun to realize that industrial waste from Japan and North America is dangerously contaminating fishing resources that are not as inexhaustible as their grandparents once believed.

More than ever, we need to understand that there is an intimate connection between the economics of development and the environment. Only by inquiring deeply into this interdisciplinary relationship may we start to assert the environmental threat in its full dimension and frame the necessary policies for our survival.

Although ecology and economics derive from the same Greek root—*oikos*, meaning household—until recently these disciplines shared relatively little of their respective analytical frameworks. Contacts between ecology and economics were sporadic, and their scopes of analysis were considered completely separate and distinct. This is no longer so. There is a fundamental relationship between these disciplines, given the exchanges that occur between complex communities of producers and consumers. Nothing is given away for free; everything is sold. This simple statement is part of an important paradigm shift that is taking place in economics: the transition from an economy based on a perception of infinite resources to one based on an understanding of environmental limits, from cowboy or frontier economics to the "economics of the coming spaceship Earth," as Kenneth Boulding ably stated it over a quarter century ago.

Until recently, economists were taught that air and water were free goods provided by nature in unlimited quantities. Environmental functions or services, such as water and nutrient cycling or climate regulation, were easily dismissed because, since there were no markets for them, they fell outside the price system and were essentially priced at zero. Natural capital was not treated as a conventional form of capital and thus its depreciation and maintenance requirements were not included in economic calculations.

Little attention was paid to the role of the environment, either as a resource base or as a "sink" to receive the residues of production and consumption activities. Traditionally, economists have neglected the effects of production and consumption activities on the environment and considered these side effects externalities. Today, we have become keenly aware that these inevitable effects of economic undertakings cannot be considered external, for someone always has to bear the "external" costs.

The paradigm that is emerging is based on a broader view of economic activity that pays greater attention to the physical and biological environment within which production and consumption take place. Within this framework, environmental costs must be internalized rather than transferred to others or to future generations. Since the new paradigm is based on the internalization of full costs, it is essential to assess both costs and benefits accurately and to distinguish clearly between true income generation and the erosion of natural capital through resource depletion or degradation.

An important concept was introduced in 1987 when the

United Nations Commission on Environment and Development issued its report. The Brundtland Report, as it became known, after Norwegian Prime Minister Gro Harlem Brundtland, who chaired the Commission, coined the term "sustainable development" to refer to the development options of future generations. This simple definition caught on rapidly, and during the past five years the concept of sustainability has gained widespread acceptance and become part of the vocabulary of almost all political leaders and policy makers. The United Nations Conference on Environment and Development (UNCED), which took place in Rio de Janeiro in June 1992 under the wise and inspired leadership of Maurice Strong, is an important example of this trend. Over one hundred heads of state from every corner of the planet gave support to the concept of sustainable development. If the environment was introduced as a global issue at the United Nations 1972 Stockholm conference, it is undeniable that environmentalism and the search for sustainable development came of age at the Earth Summit in Rio.

Unfortunately, the economic implications of sustainability are not yet sufficiently clear to policy makers and economic practitioners. In *Green Markets*, Theodore Panayotou presents fundamental economic arguments that explain the roots of environmental degradation and help in the design of appropriate policies to redirect development efforts toward a sustainable course.

The author first focuses on the economic causes of environmental damage and then explains the reforms necessary to move toward sustainable development, including the elimination of disincentives, correction of market failures, and policy reform. Given that sustainability requires concern for the future, it is necessary to consider long-term resource productivity and long-run costs and benefits. Panayotou clearly notes that decision makers tend to consider only the short-term benefits, while ignoring the long-term costs. This tendency leads to the conversion of forests to pastures or wastelands with few current benefits and enormous future costs.

Panayotou focuses on the fact that many environmental services and resources fall outside the present configuration of markets, and since they are left outside this domain, they remain unowned, unpriced, and unaccounted for in economic terms. In the worst cases, subsidies tend to accelerate excessive destruction despite growing scarcity and rising social costs.

Green Markets considers market and policy failures separately. It also analyzes the relationships between these failures and the reforms necessary to achieve sustainable economic development. Panayotou draws on his wide international experience and supports his arguments with concrete case studies.

In the aftermath of the UNCED process, the world urgently needs an effort to define sustainable development in operational terms, and this work makes an important contribution toward elucidating the economic and policy aspects of sustainability. The volume is essential reading for policy makers and economic practitioners alike in developing and industrial nations.

It is said that when Hernándo Cortes, the conquistador of Mexico, contemplated Tenochtitlán—the capital of the Aztecs—from afar, he was captivated by its beauty. Cradled in the midst of a high plateau was a shining, silvery lake that sparkled with the early morning sun. In the lake sat an island, and on the island the powerful heart of the Mexican Empire palpitated.

What Cortes did not see, however, were the depleted forests in the foothills that descended from the snow-covered volcanos into the valley. Nor was he aware, as his soldiers marched along the Tacuba causeway into the Plaza Mayor, of the polluted waters that kissed its shores. Cortes, blinded by a mirage of greatness, was unable to perceive the ecological degradation that surrounded him.

Let us not be like Cortes, for whom the glory of Tenochtitlán was apparent only in its priceless treasures. Instead, let us foresee the world to come as an opportunity to share and celebrate the most valuable of all gifts: life—life that can be abundant and enduring only through solidarity and respect for our natural heritage.

Oscar Arias
Former president of Costa Rica
Nobel Peace Prize laureate

San José, Costa Rica
December 1992

Preface

Environmental issues have played an important part in the news in recent years, and the public debate has tended to focus on trade-offs between conservation and economic growth. The belief has been that in order to grow countries have no choice but to deplete their resources, saving environmental concerns for a later, wealthier stage of development. After reaping the rewards of growth, they can spend their riches remedying the environmental degradation created along the way. Developing countries, faced with environmental demands from the industrial world, have naturally responded that they cannot yet afford the luxury of environmentalism.

Environmental economists, however, tend to look at the environment as an integral part of genuine growth. In this view, economic growth requires concern for the future as well as the present, and development is not genuine if it is not sustainable.

Green Markets is the third volume in the cooperative publication effort of ICEG and HIID and the seventh in ICEG's series of Sector Studies, which examine developing countries' responses to specific policy problems. Here, Theodore Panayotou presents clear and thoughtful analysis on how economics both explains environmental degradation and suggests solutions. The key is the proper valuation of resources.

Using abundant examples of success and failure, Panayotou makes the case that environmental degradation at the current rate is bad economics—but there is a solution. Government policies, he points out, often unwittingly create and exacerbate environmental degradation, because they generally do nothing to correct its root causes. What governments must do, and what some have done successfully, is to create market conditions for environmental resources. Panayotou shows that simply by pricing irrigation water appropriately, for instance, governments could increase agricultural yields, manage scarce water more efficiently, improve equity among farmers, and gain revenues. Everyone would benefit.

Panayotou, a foremost natural resource economist with HIID, has advised governments around the world about how to preserve their environments while pursuing development. Drawing on his experience and research, he explains how sustainable development works in concrete terms, giving suggestions for reform in developing countries and for new approaches by aid agencies.

Nicolás Ardito-Barletta
General Director
International Center
for Economic Growth
Panama City, Panama

Dwight H. Perkins
Director
Harvard Institute for
International Development
Cambridge, Massachusetts

February 1993

Acknowledgments

This study was made possible in part by the financial assistance of the U.S. Agency for International Development through the Consulting Assistance on Economic Reform Project at the Harvard Institute for International Development. I wish to thank Mona Yacoubian and Madeleine Hirschland for their assistance in the preparation of the cases. I also appreciate the comments and suggestions of several colleagues and readers of an earlier version. I remain, however, ultimately responsible for any errors and omissions.

T. P.

About the Author

Theodore Panayotou is a fellow at the Harvard Institute for International Development and a lecturer in the Department of Economics at Harvard University. A specialist in environmental and resource economics, environmental policy analysis, and development economics, Dr. Panayotou has advised governments and institutes in Asia, Africa, and Eastern Europe, as well as numerous other national and international institutions, on the interactions between the natural resource base and economic development. Dr. Panayotou served for a decade as visiting professor and resident adviser in Southeast Asia, and recently cowrote a multivolume environmental policy study at the Thailand Development Research Institute in Bangkok. The author of several books, including *Not by Timber Alone: Economics and Ecology for Sustaining Tropical Forests* (with Peter S. Ashton, Island Press, 1992), and numerous articles and monographs, he is currently at work on another book, *Natural Resources, Environment, and Development: Economics, Policy, and Management*. Dr. Panayotou received the 1991 Distinguished Achievement Award of the Society for Conservation Biology for his wide-ranging efforts to use economic analysis as a tool for conservation.

Nature never gives anything to anyone; everything is sold. It is only in the abstraction of ideals that choice comes without consequences.

—*Ralph Waldo Emerson*

CHAPTER 1

Environmental Degradation: The Magnitude of the Problem

Few problems are as common to all countries, regardless of economic system and level of development, as environmental degradation. This degradation is more pervasive in the developing world than high inflation, excessive foreign debt, or economic stagnation. Rapid deforestation, watershed degradation, loss of biological diversity, fuelwood and water shortages, water contamination, excessive soil erosion, land degradation, overgrazing and overfishing, air pollution, and urban congestion are as common in rapidly growing Southeast Asia as they are in stagnating sub-Saharan Africa and heavily indebted Latin America. Although economic growth potentially enables countries to deal more effectively with environmental problems, experience so far has yielded an abundance of failures and a scarcity of successes.

These observations have several implications. First, there are underlying causes of environmental degradation that are common to countries in different geographical locations with different cultures and at different levels of development. Second, economic growth by itself neither causes nor remedies environmental degradation; the connections are far more subtle and complex. Third, environmental problems are insidious and refractory, or at least poorly understood, resulting either in neglect or in interventions that treat the symptoms rather than the underlying causes.

Environmental degradation is taking place at cumulative rates that, if left unchecked, will ultimately undermine economic growth. For this reason, environmental protection is not a luxury of concern only to industrial countries, but is crucial for developing countries as well. Calls for environmental protection based simply on rates of deforestation, soil erosion, or air pollution, however, are misguided. As I will attempt to show in this book, the physical manifestations of environmental degradation are lagging and misleading indicators of unsustainable development. Rather, the *economic* manifestations of environmental degradation are the most useful indicators for those who wish to pursue sustainable development, for they suggest both the root causes of and possible remedies for environmental degradation.

Ultimately, excessive environmental damage can be traced to "bad" economics stemming from misguided government policies and distorted markets that set inappropriate prices for natural resources. Sustainable development, therefore, requires that government correct these market failures and reform policies. Despite the apparent short-term trade-offs, good economics and good environment go hand-in-hand, especially in developing countries, where there is great potential for improving the efficiency with which resources are allocated and used.

In this book I will explain how bad economics works to encourage environmental degradation and thereby threatens economic growth. Although failed attempts to protect resources abound, there have also been successes that offer hope for progress and models for emulation and adaptation. This book will examine both the failures and the successes, which are instructive for policy makers in developing countries, for bilateral and multilateral assistance agencies, and for environmental groups that hope to bring about sustainable development. The book will address the issue of the proper role of the market and the government in preserving the environment. I will also explain how sound economic policy, designed to correct distorted markets, can work to the benefit of both the environment and the economy, setting a country on a path of sustainable development.

I will begin by presenting a way of understanding and evaluating environmental degradation.

Physical Manifestations of Environmental Degradation

The term "environment" refers to both the quantity and quality of natural resources, renewable and nonrenewable. It also includes the ambient environment, which consists of the landscape, water, air, and the atmosphere and constitutes an essential element of the quality of life. Defined as such, the environment is a critical determinant of the quantity, quality, and sustainability of human activities and life in general. Environmental degradation then is the diminution of the environment in quantity and its deterioration in quality.

Correspondingly, environmental problems have both a quantity and a quality dimension. Water-related problems include water shortages as well as deterioration of water quality through pollution and contamination. Forest-related problems include both deforestation, in the sense of forest cover loss, and forest degradation, in the sense of reduced forest productivity, loss of diversity, and replacement of primary by secondary forest. Land-related problems include growing land scarcity as well as soil erosion, nutrient leaching, waterlogging, and salinization. Fishery-related problems include overfishing as well as changes in species composition to less valuable species, an increasing share of lower-quality fish in the catch, and fish contamination. Urban environmental problems include congestion and hence less open space available per person, as well as air, water, and noise pollution.

As quality problems become severe, they turn into quantity problems. For example, water may become completely unusable because of heavy pollution. Land may become unsuitable for cultivation because of severe erosion. A forest area may completely lose its forest cover because of severe degradation; this occurs, for example, when a shortening of the fallow cycle in a system of shifting cultivation results in the replacement of forest by *imperata* grass, a weed that is very costly to eliminate.[1] Certain urban areas (such as slums and residential areas near dumpsites and chemical or nuclear plants) may become unlivable because of excessive pollution and contamination. Quality problems also become quantity problems because quantity is limited for a given quality. For example, shortages of drinking water, prime farmland, and primary forests may coexist with abundance of low-quality water, marginal land, and secondary forests.

Finally, diversity has value. Expanding the supply of one resource or environment at the expense of another may be beneficial up to a point, but as any given resource is driven to depletion or extinction, diversity is lost, and with it a development option and an element of the quality of life. Diversity of species and environments is essential to long-term productivity and sustainability of economic development. Its preservation is a form of investment for the future or insurance against future uncertainties. Its diminution constitutes environmental degradation even if an equally productive asset has replaced it as a factor of production or a source of consumption. In conclusion, when speaking of environmental degradation, it is important to keep in mind its three dimensions—quantity, quality, and diversity—and their interdependence.

The Economics of Environmental Degradation

A certain level of environmental degradation is an inevitable consequence of human activity. Any exploitation of nonrenewable resources inevitably results in their partial or total depletion, as well as in the degradation of the landscape and the generation of waste. Industrialization leads to increased consumption of minerals and energy and the generation of air, water, and noise pollution and hazardous wastes. Agricultural extensification (increasing productivity by increasing cultivated area) leads to deforestation, cultivation of marginal lands, and soil erosion, while agricultural intensification (increasing productivity by increasing the amount of capital and labor employed) leads to pesticide and fertilizer runoffs, waterlogging, and soil salinity. Even the use of renewable resources on a sustainable basis presupposes the mining of the stock down to a level that would generate maximum annual growth (or maximum sustainable yield). Virgin fisheries and undisturbed forests reach a natural equilibrium stock where net growth is zero; unless the stock is reduced, there is no sustainable yield to harvest. Therefore, some environmental degradation is inevitable.

The question is not how to prevent or eliminate environmental degradation altogether but how to minimize it or at least to keep it to a level consistent with society's objectives. When environmental degradation is seen in the context of the society's development objectives, not all deforestation, soil erosion, or water pollution is worth preventing. Some deforestation is necessary and beneficial when the forest land is put to a superior use, which may be agricultural, industrial, or residential. As long as all costs, including those arising from diminished quantity and quality and lost diversity of forests, have been accounted for; as long as both the productivity and the sustainability of the alternative uses have been considered with a due margin of error; and as long as any side effects of the forest conversion have been paid for by those who generated them, deforestation should be acceptable.

The problem is that decision makers usually consider the short-term benefits of forest conversion but not the long-term costs. As a result, too much conversion takes place in areas where the present value of costs outweighs any short-term benefits. Even worse, forests are converted to wastelands with little current benefit and enormous current and future costs. It renders a disservice to conservation when such wasteful forest destruction is lumped together with socially optimal forest conversion into a single deforestation figure. Considering the rate at which tropical forests have been disappearing in recent years, however, it is understandable that all deforestation is considered undesirable, no matter what the economic justification (see Table 1). Nevertheless, this emphasis on the symptoms rather than on the underlying causes and the disregard of the costs and benefits involved prevent the formulation of effective policies to deal with the problem. At the same time

TABLE 1

Deforestation in Selected Tropical Countries, 1980–1985

Country	Closed forest area in 1980 (thousands of hectares)	Average annual rate of deforestation, 1981–1985 (percentage)
Group 1		
Malaysia	20,996	1.2
Thailand	9,235	2.6
Philippines	9,510	1.0
Nepal	1,941	4.1
Nigeria	5,950	5.0
Ivory Coast	4,458	6.5
Group 2		
Brazil	357,480	0.4
Indonesia	113,895	0.5
India	51,841	0.3
Group 3		
Kenya	1,105	1.0
Mozambique	935	1.1
Group 4		
Pakistan	2,185	0.0
Ethiopia	4,350	0.1
Central African Republic	3,590	0.1

NOTE: Table gives data for selected countries from each group. Group 1 countries have higher than average rates of deforestation and large areas affected. Group 2 countries have relatively low rates but large areas affected. Group 3 countries have high rates and small areas of forest affected. Group 4 countries have low or moderate rates and small areas affected.

SOURCE: Robert Repetto, *The Forest for the Trees? Government Policies and the Misuse of Forest Resources* (Washington, D.C.: World Resources Institute, 1988).

these attitudes antagonize developing countries that depend on forest resources for development.

A similar case can be made for soil erosion and water pollution. Not all soil erosion is worth preventing. In deep fertile soils, erosion has little or no effect on land productivity, while it enhances considerably the productivity of downstream land where it is deposited. Still, erosion may have other negative offsite effects, such as sedimentation and eutrophication of waterways and reservoirs, that should be taken into account in determining how much soil erosion to allow. In other areas, such as in many of the tropical rain forests, where the fertile soil is very superficial, consisting basically of the humus formed by degrading matter, any soil loss may make the difference between lush growth and desertification. Again the tendency is to lump together all soil erosion and express it in tons per hectare without regard to the depth of soil, fertility, natural replenishment, and deposition.

Similarly, air and water pollution are excessive not in an absolute sense but in relation to the capacity of these media to assimilate emissions and effluents and in reference to society's constraints and objectives. To attempt to prevent all forms and levels of pollution in all water resources is to leave unused a resource with little opportunity cost (forgone alternative use), thereby reducing social welfare or requiring the use of resources with a higher opportunity cost for the same purpose. This does not imply that individuals should be allowed to use the assimilative capacity of the environment free of charge. If they do, not only will excessive pollution be generated but the resource itself—that is, the assimilative capacity of the environment—will also be diminished. Moreover, as the disposal of waste increases and the assimilative capacity is reduced, individual users should pay an opportunity cost consisting of two elements: (1) the cost of using a scarce resource to the exclusion of other uses and (2) the cost of damage to the productivity of the resource as waste disposal increases beyond a certain threshold. A charge for the use of the resource can be set high enough to limit effluents to a level that can be assimilated without damage to its assimilative capacity.

Prevention is often far more cost-effective than rehabilitation. Once excessive environmental degradation takes place, it is not worthwhile to attempt to reduce it back to the level that would have been optimal with prevention because costs are higher, effectiveness is lower, and vested interests stronger. Not only is 100 percent abatement technically difficult and economically out of the question, but the economically optimal level of pollution abatement would unavoidably leave us with more pollution than we would have liked had we had the option of a fresh start. Because of this economic irreversibility (which sets in well before physical irreversibility), prompt internalization of environmental costs is both economically and environmentally preferable. Environmental costs are internalized when they are borne by those who generate them rather than by innocent bystanders or the society at large, as is usually the case at present.

To sum up, physical manifestations of environmental degradation, such as rates of deforestation and soil erosion and levels of water pollution and urban density, tend to overstate the problem, because they seem to suggest that all degradation is preventable or worth abating. Because they are based on observed symptoms rather than underlying causes, they tend to be devoid of analytical insight about how to deal with the problem, other than banning the activities that appear to be responsible. For example, if logging leads to deforestation, it is common sense that banning logging will solve the problem. As Thailand is gradually discovering, however, a logging ban does not stop logging (let alone deforestation), any more than Prohibition in the United States several decades ago stopped drinking.

Economic Manifestations of Environmental Degradation

The first step in understanding the root causes of environmental degradation is to look for its economic manifestations. Examining the economic manifestations of environmental degradation can help define the true dimension of the problem and suggest the best approach to cost-effective intervention. Economic manifestations are counterintuitive observations or contradictions. Their very identification calls for an analytical explanation and has implications for policy. The following is a representative list of such economic manifestations of environmental degradation:

1. *Overuse, waste, and inefficiency coexist with growing resource scarcity and shortages.*

For example, increasingly scarce irrigation water in many parts of Asia is used wastefully and excessively by some farmers to the point of causing waterlogging and salinization of soils, while other farmers in the same irrigation system suffer from water shortages and unreliable supplies. This is true of most irrigation systems in Thailand, Indonesia, Philippines, India, and Pakistan, to mention only a few (see Case 1 on page 10). The net loss consists of current production loss by those who receive inadequate water and future production loss by those who suffer from waterlogging as well as general degradation of the resource.

2. *An increasingly scarce resource is put to inferior, low-return, and unsustainable uses, when superior, high-return, and sustainable uses exist.*

In Thailand, for example, uplands suitable for fruit trees or other perennials are often planted with maize or cassava for a few years and abandoned as yields decline. Perennials would both yield higher returns (in present value terms) and be more sustainable. In Morocco scarce irrigation water is used to grow sugarcane in an arid environment, when vegetables, fruits, and other higher-value crops would have produced a higher return and fewer soil salinity problems. In Brazil, valuable forests have been converted to ranches that generate negative economic returns (see Case 2 on page 14).

3. *A renewable resource capable of sustainable management is exploited as an extractive resource (in other words, it is mined).*

Tropical forests are being mined without concern for regeneration and future harvests, even when future harvests have a positive net present value at the market rate of interest (see Case 3 on page 18). Although some forest land conversion to other uses is economically justifiable, the fact that the rate of deforestation is 100 times the rate of reforestation suggests that tropical forests are being mined, not managed. There are indeed few sustainable alternatives that would justify failure to regenerate a renewable resource capable of yielding a perpetual stream of income.

4. *A resource is put to a single use when multiple uses would generate a larger net benefit.*

Many tropical forests, for example, are managed for timber production alone when management for multiple uses such as nontimber goods, water and soil conservation, biological diversity, and a host of other environmental services would generate a higher return (see Case 3). Although not all uses are mutually

CASE 1

Policy Failure: Irrigation Water in Developing Countries

From India to Morocco to Botswana, free or heavily subsidized irrigation water obstructs market signals, encouraging farmers to use the resource beyond its economic and agricultural optimum. Underpriced water also stifles incentives to invest in maintaining and improving existing dams, which are often plagued by poor drainage and inefficient distribution systems. In Bangladesh, Nepal, and Thailand, total costs of supplying water were at least 1,000 percent of revenues collected.

Cheap water often becomes a substitute for other inputs, such as land improvement and soil conservation. Overirrigation by farmers closest to the water source leads to waterlogging, salinization, and alkalization of soil. The consequences are reduced crop yields, reduced fertility of irrigated lands, and increased salt loadings of aquifers and return flows (the surplus water returning to the water source after passing through a farmer's land). Downstream effects include the erosion and siltation of estuaries and deltas.

Meanwhile, those less conveniently located are forced to rely on sporadic and sparse water supplies. A study of Pakistani irrigation systems found that 73 percent of farmers surveyed complained of insufficient water supplies.

Water subsidies encourage farmers to treat water as an abundant resource when it is in fact scarce. With no water rights and no effective water-user associations or other mechanisms to allocate water efficiently, water scarcity does not register. Indeed, water charges do not reflect the increasing opportunity cost of water that stems from increasing scarcity.

Beyond the less apparent economic costs, there is an absence of effective financial cost-recovery mechanisms. Even at low maintenance levels, only a fraction of operation and maintenance costs is covered by the revenues collected by water users. For example, revenues cover 20 percent of costs in Bangladesh, 27 percent in Thailand, and 60 percent in Nepal. If capital costs are included, water charges often cover only 10–20 percent of costs.[1]

Underpricing of irrigation water also leads to both inefficient use and inadequate maintenance of irrigation systems, resulting in problems such as poor drainage, which in turn leads to salinization and waterlogging. The Food and Agriculture Organization (FAO) estimates that 50 percent of all irrigated lands have been damaged from salinization, alkalization, and waterlogging. In Pakistan, half the area served by the Indus Basin canal system is waterlogged, saline, or both. The same is true for the lower Rafactain Euphrates Valley in Iraq. Maintenance problems also often result in inefficient use, with as much as 75 percent of water seeping out or evaporating from unlined or obstructed canals and distributories.

The market failure inherent in underpriced water and the policy failure of irrigation subsidies and inefficient water use are inextricably linked. It is estimated that if Pakistan's irrigation system increased its efficiency by 10 percent, the water saved could irrigate another 2 million hectares.[2] As long as farmers do not bear the true cost of water, however, they are unlikely to appreciate its scarcity or recognize the problems that arise with overuse. Until they receive clear market signals indicating otherwise, they will continue to use water wastefully.

---

1. Peter Rogers, "Fresh Water," in Robert Repetto, ed., *The Global Possible: Resources, Development and the New Century* (New Haven: Yale University Press, 1985).
2. World Resources Institute and International Institute for Environment and Development, *World Resources 1987* (New York: Basic Books, 1987).

compatible, the relevant issue is which combination of uses would produce the highest net present value for a given forest.

5. *Investments in the protection and enhancement of the resource base are not undertaken, even though they would generate a positive net present value by increasing productivity and enhancing sustainability.*

Examples include the failure of many farmers throughout Asia and Africa to invest in land development and soil conservation to reduce erosion and improve irrigation. Another example is the failure of many forest concessionaires to regenerate or replant their concessions, or even to protect them from encroachment. A third example is the failure of irrigation authorities to invest in watershed protection to guard reservoirs from sedimentation and in maintenance and rehabilitation of deteriorating irrigation systems to increase their efficiency and prolong their economic life.

6. *A larger amount of effort and cost is incurred when a smaller amount of effort and cost would have generated a higher level of output, more profit, and less damage to the resource.*

Examples include fisheries and common pastures throughout the developing and parts of the developed world. Most fisheries employ twice as much labor and capital as needed to obtain less than the maximum sustainable yield and virtually no economic surplus. Any profit that the fishery is capable of generating is dissipated by excessive fishing costs. Fishermen tend to be among the lowest income groups in most countries. In the long run, overfishing decreases productivity of the stocks, lowers output, and changes the composition of the stock toward lower-value species.[2] Nor is the excessive employment a benefit in itself, because fishermen are earning no more than their opportunity costs (what they could earn in alternative employment). If they did earn more, the entry of additional workers into fishing would nullify any income differential between the fishermen and comparable socioeconomic groups in the country. A reduction in the fishing effort would reduce fishing costs and increase profits in the short run and help the stock and catch recover over the long run, leading to further increases in profits. The economic surplus so generated could be used to compensate, retrain, and reemploy the surplus fishermen. Despite these obvious gains, no such reform takes place.

The situation with common, or open-access, pastures is similar.[3] More animals are grazed than the pastures can support, with the result that total output is less than it could be, incomes are low, and the pastures deteriorate. Incomes and output can be raised and pastures improved with a reduction in the number of animals, but this does not happen. It is as if the society is subsidizing the degradation of its resource base by raising and grazing an excessive number of animals. Of course, the problem arises from the fact that the sum of individual actions does not lead to socially desirable outcomes under the prevailing institutional arrangements. Since the pasture is a common property and livestock is viewed as a transformer of common property into private property, the more animals each individual has, the larger his share of the common property, assuming that others do not also expand their herds. But since the other common owners would not sit and watch their share fall, they also increase their herds. The end result is neither efficient nor equitable. The productivity of the pasture declines, and the largest share goes to those who can afford the largest number of animals, that is, those who are initially better off. The poor suffer in what appears to be an equitable arrangement: property (and poverty) that is freely accessible to all.

7. *Local communities and tribal and other groups such as women are displaced and deprived of their customary rights of access to resources, regardless of the fact that by their very presence or because of their specialized knowledge, traditions, and self-interest they may be the most cost-effective managers of the resource.*

Many tropical resources, particularly the rain forests, are so complex and vulnerable that their sustainable management requires specialized knowledge of plants and animals and how they interact with each other and their environment. It also requires a physical presence to prevent encroachment or other interference by those less knowledgeable or less interested in

CASE 2

Policy Failure: Ranching for Subsidies in Brazil

In the 1960s, the Brazilian government introduced extensive legislation aimed at developing the Amazon region. Over the next two decades, a combination of new fiscal and financial incentives encouraged the conversion of forest to pasture land. During the 1970s, some 8,000–10,000 square kilometers of forest were cleared for pasture each year. The proportion of land used for pasture in the Amazonian state of Rondonia increased from 2.5 percent in 1970 to 25.6 percent in 1985.[1]

It is now clear that transforming the Amazon into ranchland is both economically unsound and environmentally harmful. Without tree cover, the fragile Amazonian soil often loses its fertility, and at least 20 percent of the pastures may be at some stage of deterioration.[2] Indeed, cattle ranching is considered one of the foremost proximate causes of deforestation. Furthermore, ranching provides few long-term employment opportunities. Livestock projects offer work only during the initial slash-and-burn phase. Negative employment effects have been observed when income-generating tree crops such as Brazil nuts are eradicated for pasture.[3]

Nonetheless, the incentives designed to attract ranching, which were administered by the government's Superintendency for the Development of the Amazon (SUDAM), were powerful. Fiscal incentives included ten- to fifteen-year tax holidays, investment tax credits (ITCs), and export tax or import duty exemptions. ITCs allowed corporations to exempt 50 percent of their tax liabilities by investing their savings in SUDAM–approved projects.[4] SUDAM evaluated projects and financed up to 75 percent of the investment costs of those that received favorable ratings using tax credit funds.

Starting in 1974, subsidized credit also played a crucial role in encouraging numerous ranching projects. The Program of Agricultural, Livestock and Mineral Poles in Amazonia (POLAMAZONIA) offered ranchers loans at 12 percent interest, while market interest rates were at 45 percent. Subsidized loans of 49–76 percent of face value were typical through the early 1980s.[5] The program discriminated against poor tenant farmers who lacked the necessary collateral. Also, tax breaks and cheap money were capitalized into the land, making property more expensive and even less accessible to the poor.[6]

The subsidies and tax breaks encouraged ranchers to undertake projects that would not otherwise have been profitable. A World Resources Institute study showed that the typical subsidized investment yielded an economic loss equal to 55 percent of the initial investment. If subsidies received by the private investor are taken into account, however, the typical investment yielded a positive financial return equal to 250 percent of the initial outlay. (For a detailed calculation of financial and economic returns from government-assisted ranches in the Brazilian Amazon, see Table A1 in Appendix A.) The fiscal and financial incentives masked what were intrinsically poor investments and served to subsidize the conversion of a superior asset (tropical forest) into an inferior use (cattle ranching). Moreover, a survey of SUDAM projects reveals that five projects received tax credit funds without even being implemented.[7]

---

1. Dennis J. Mahar, *Government Policies and Deforestation in Brazil's Amazon Region* (Washington, D.C.: World Bank, 1989).

2. Robert Repetto, "Economic Policy Reform for Natural Resource Conservation," Environment Working Paper (Washington, D.C.: World Bank, May 1988).

3. Mahar, *Government Policies and Deforestation in Brazil's Amazon Region*.

4. After 1974 these exemptions were limited to 25 percent of tax liabilities.

5. Robert Repetto, *The Forest for the Trees? Government Policies and the Misuse of Forest Resources* (Washington, D.C.: World Resources Institute, 1988).

6. Subsidized credit was eliminated completely by mid-1987.

7. Mahar, *Government Policies and Deforestation in Brazil's Amazon Region*.

the continued productivity and sustainability of the resource. Managers that combine such specialized knowledge with a personal commitment to the long-term sustainability of the resource and a willingness to live in the rain forest, far from the city lights, are hard to find. Even if they existed, employing an adequate number of them with all the necessary support would be prohibitively expensive.

Fortunately, there are people who live in the forest, depend on it for survival, have the specialized knowledge necessary to manage the ecosystem in a sustainable way, and even have a tradition of doing so. By any criterion, such as cost-effectiveness, present value maximization, or equity, many local communities and tribal groups ought to be given the responsibility of managing the resource and vested with sufficient authority, protection, and security of tenure to do so effectively. Yet, in most cases, central governments have themselves assumed the ownership and management of tropical forests despite their lack of specialized knowledge and management skills, their absenteeism, and often their lack of interest in the sustainability of the resource. The rights of exploitation have subsequently been awarded to equally distant logging companies who have little knowledge of the rain forest environment and no interest or stake in its long-term productivity and sustainability. Short-term concessions and perverse taxation have not helped either. In the meantime, local communities have been deprived of their customary rights of access or displaced altogether.

Under these circumstances, it is no wonder that tropical forests are being destroyed by the combined actions of logging firms that seek short-term profits and local communities that seek a livelihood without a secure resource base. Neither group has an assurance of a share in the future of the resource. For example, African women who are responsible for managing resources but lack access to secure property rights, extension, and credit have no choice but to overuse land and to farm areas that should not be cultivated. Encroachment on the resource by farmers and ranchers in search of land for agriculture and cattle ranching further compounds the uncertainty and effectively reduces state ownership of open-access land. Unlike most developing country governments, which have declared state ownership over all forest resources with little consideration of local customary rights, the government of Papua New Guinea recognizes and defends communal and tribal tenure over land and forest resources (see Case 4 on page 20).

8. *Public projects are undertaken that do not make adequate provisions or generate sufficient benefits to compensate all those affected (including the environment) sufficiently to make them decidedly better off with that project than without it.*

Public projects aim to increase total welfare or to promote economic development, not to effect a redistribution of income, although, other things being equal, projects that benefit the poor more than the rich ought to be preferred. Therefore, public projects should fully compensate all those affected, including future generations. If a project is truly beneficial, it ought to generate sufficient benefits to make all those involved or affected better off with the project than without the project through actual, not hypothetical, compensation. This should be so especially since those affected more severely are usually the poor, who lack the political and economic power to avoid being harmed. The analysis of who is affected by public projects should be broken down by location, income level, profession, and gender. Such a breakdown will help ensure that the effects on disadvantaged segments of society are not neglected, as is often the case.

In addition, the expected benefits from the project ought to be sufficient to mitigate or compensate for the project's environmental effects so that the country's environment is not decidedly worse off with the project than without the project. For example, if a forest area is inundated by the construction of a dam, an equivalent area of forest must be created elsewhere (for instance, by purchasing logging rights from concession companies or through extensive replanting with similar species).

Many irrigation projects fail to meet these conditions and thus create social tensions and long delays that result in cost overruns and forgone benefits, if indeed they are beneficial overall. Examples abound. The Narmada irrigation and hydroelectric project in India, for instance, has been delayed for some thirty years because of local resistance. If such projects do go

CASE 3

*Evaluating a Tropical Forest for Multiple Use:
The Mishana Forest in Peru*

Tropical forests capable of generating a multitude of products and services are often exploited commercially for a single use such as timber production, or they are converted to plantation or ranching use even though management for multiple uses would generate a higher net present value. A recent study has calculated the net present value of forest products in a one-hectare stand of the Mishana Forest on the Rio Nanay, twenty kilometers southwest of Iquitos, Peru.[1] It found that managing the forest for a combination of fruits, latex, and timber would generate a net present value three times as high as that of converting to an intensively managed single-species plantation.

A systematic inventory of a single hectare of forest showed 50 families, 275 species, and 842 individual trees of less than ten centimeters in diameter, of which 73 species (26.2 percent) and 350 individuals (41.6 percent) yielded products that have market value in Iquitos. Seven tree species and 4 palm species produced edible fruits, 60 species were commercial timber trees, and 2 species produced rubber.

The study assessed the actual market value of the forest resources, including fruit, timber, and rubber, and determined the yield of useful products per unit of time for each resource. The net revenues generated by the sale of each resource were calculated based on current market values and the costs associated with harvesting and transportation. Two different harvest scenarios were used. The first involved the selective removal of all existing timber of greater than thirty centimeters in diameter in year 0, year 20, and year 40, with a final cut of all remaining trees (pro-jected to have a minimum diameter of thirty centimeters) in year 65. Annual collections of fruit and latex were conducted throughout the sixty-five-year cutting cycle. The second scenario, a sustainable yield scheme, assumed selective timber removal (thirty cubic meters per harvest) on a twenty-year cutting cycle, with annual fruit and latex collections in perpetuity.

Using the criteria for the first scenario, the native plant resources on the site possessed a net present value (NPV) of US$9,191.77 (fruit, US$7,679.81; latex, US$428.39; timber, US$1,083.57). Using the second scenario, the NPV comes to US$8,610.13 (fruit, US$8,002.60; latex, US$446.40; timber, US$161.13). It is important to note that in this latter scenario, fruit represents 92.9 percent, and fruit and latex together, the "minor forest products," 98.1 percent of the total NPV of the forest.

The NPV calculations for the Mishana forest demonstrate that natural forest use is economically competitive with other forms of land use in the tropics. Using identical investment criteria, the NPV of the timber and pulpwood obtained from an intensively managed plantation of *Gmelina arborea* in Brazilian Amazonia is estimated at US$3,184, and gross revenues from fully stocked cattle pastures in Brazil are reported to be US$148 per hectare per year, with an NPV of US$2,960. Thus, even though multiple-use management of this tropical forest could generate three times the net present value of a single-species, single-use plantation, large tracts of forests in Peruvian and Brazilian Amazonia are converted to such plantations and ranches.

---

1. Material for this case is taken from C. M. Peters, A. H. Gentry, and R. Mendelsohn, "Valuation of a Tropical Forest in Peruvian Amazonia," *Nature* 339 (1989).

CASE 4

Policy Success: Communal Tenure in Papua New Guinea

Unlike most of the developing world, Papua New Guinea has maintained its communal tenure customs while adapting to the requirements of an increasingly market-oriented economy. While the latter requires clear land ownership, Papua New Guinea's experience has shown that converting land from communal to freehold ownership may confuse rather than clarify the rights of ownership. The widespread land degradation encouraged by the insecure tenure, loss of entitlements, and open access characteristic of state-owned land elsewhere has been absent from Papua New Guinea.

Most countries have responded to market pressures for clear ownership by imposing a new system of private or state ownership. In contrast, Papua New Guinea's land law builds upon the customs governing its communally held land. The country's Land Ordinance Act calls for local mediators and land courts to base settlements on existing principles of communal ownership. Consequently, 97 percent of the land remains communal, has been neither surveyed nor registered, and is governed by local custom.[1]

This communal tenure seems to provide clearer ownership rights, with all their environmental and market implications, than private ownership. Settlements that convert communal land to freehold are often later disputed, and reversion back to customary ownership is a frequent outcome. Yet unlike state-owned land in other developing countries, communal land in Papua New Guinea is neither in effect unowned nor public. Rather, the bundle of rights deemed "ownership" in the West does not reside in one party. For example, individual families hold the right to farm plots of land indefinitely, but the right to trade them resides in the clan.[2]

The island's communal systems have long resulted in the sustainable use of its more densely populated highlands. Even with a nine-thousand-year agricultural history, a wet climate, and population growth of at least 2.3 percent, the highlands remain fertile. The population, which is primarily agricultural, enjoys a per capita income more than twice that of El Salvador, Western Samoa, and Nigeria.[3] In marked contrast to much of the developing world, only 6 million of its 46 million hectares of forest land have been converted to other uses.[4]

The lack of deforestation comes as no surprise since those who control the land have an interest in the sustainable, productive use of the forest. Rather than dealing with a distant government in need of quick revenues and foreign exchange, companies seeking logging rights must negotiate directly with those who have secure tenure and who use the land not only to farm, but also to gather fruit, hunt, and collect materials for clothing, buildings, and weapons.[5] Because the communal tenure patterns provide an entitlement to all clan members, individuals have little incentive to sacrifice future value for current use.

---

1. Robert D. Cooter, "Inventing Property: Economic Theories of the Origins of Market Property Applied to Papua New Guinea" (Berkeley: University of California, 1990), mimeo.

2. Ibid.

3. Ibid.

4. Australian UNESCO Committee for Man and the Biosphere, *Ecological Effects of Increasing Human Activities on Tropical and Sub-Tropical Forest Ecosystems* (Canberra: Australian Government Publishing Services, 1976).

5. Theodore Panayotou and Peter S. Ashton, *Not by Timber Alone: Economics and Ecology for Sustaining Tropical Forests* (Washington, D.C.: Island Press, 1992); Australian UNESCO Committee for Man and the Biosphere, *Ecological Effects of Increasing Human Activities.*

through without meeting these conditions, they run into problems of watershed encroachment by the displaced population, sedimentation, and loss of capacity. A case in point is the Nam Pong Reservoir in northeast Thailand (see Case 5 on page 24). The Dumoga-Bone irrigation system and national park in Sulawesi, Indonesia, is a counterexample that has met the conditions for a socially beneficial and sustainable project (see Case 6 on page 28).

9. *Resources and by-products are not recycled, even when recycling would generate both economic and environmental benefits.*

With the exception of energy, the consumption of natural resource commodities such as minerals, wood products, and other fibers generates recyclable waste. Although not all recyclable waste can be recycled economically at the current levels of technology and costs, many could be profitably recycled if material from primary sources were priced appropriately and if unrecycled waste could not be disposed of free of charge. Inadequate recycling means more exploitation of natural resources, more pollution, and loss of salvageable economic value. Recycling is implicitly taxed by depletion allowances and exploration subsidies for primary resource extraction. Even when recycling is more costly than primary production, the environmental benefits from recycling (such as less waste disposal and less degradation of the environment by primary production) could help tip the balance if appropriately internalized.

A good example is palm oil processing in Sumatra, Indonesia. The residuals from palm oil production could be economically converted into fertilizer if the averted damage to the aquatic life and other uses of water were taken into account. Because factories can dispose of their waste in the rivers free of charge, however, a profitable economic activity is forgone. As a result, palm oil waste is today Sumatra's single most severe form of water pollution. Related losses include damage to the riverine and coastal fisheries and reduced water quality for household use.

10. *Unique sites and habitats are lost and animal and plant species go extinct without compelling economic reasons that counter the value of uniqueness and diversity and the cost of irreversible loss.*

As a resource becomes increasingly scarce, its social value rises regardless of whether it is traded in the market or not. The value of resources with no close substitutes, such as natural habitats and animal and plant species, approaches infinity as their numbers are reduced to levels that threaten their continued existence. Both uniqueness and the marginal contribution of threatened environments and species to diversity is of such great value that their irreversible loss and the associated loss of future options cannot be justified except in very special cases when survival is at stake, such as during famine or when enormous and indisputable economic benefits are expected. Yet unique sites and habitats and threatened species are often driven to extinction by public projects or with the help of government subsidies without compelling economic reasons to counter such enormous loss. The burden of proof that such resources have a lower value than the proposed projects or policies ought to be with those who advocate these interventions.

The Causes of Environmental Degradation

Unlike physical manifestations and symptoms, which are devoid of analytical insight, the economic manifestations of environmental degradation raise analytical questions about cause and effect. Why are increasingly scarce resources being inefficiently used and wasted instead of economized and conserved? Why are valuable resources being put to inferior uses when superior uses exist? Why are renewable resources being mined rather than managed for a perpetual stream of benefits when the latter would generate a higher net present value? Why are resources that generate a multitude of products and services being put to a single use when multiple-use management would generate more benefits? Why are highly profitable investments that would enhance both current productivity and future sustainability not being undertaken, while scarce funds

CASE 5

Policy Failure: Costs of Unplanned
Resettlement, Nam Pong Reservoir, Thailand

The Nam Pong Water Resources Project in northeast Thailand illustrates the potential effects of mismanaging the environmental aspects of water projects. The intensive resettlement of people displaced by the Nam Pong Reservoir into areas within its watershed has resulted in widespread deforestation. This, in turn, has significantly increased the level of sedimentation in the reservoir, quantifiably and substantially reducing its economic value.

The Ubolratana Dam, which created the Nam Pong Reservoir, was constructed in 1966 to regulate flooding, generate hydropower, and irrigate surrounding areas. The reservoir's estimated life was 500 years.[1] At that time, virtually all the better farmland in the surrounding area was under cultivation, 85 percent of the inhabitants were farmers, and the population growth rate was 3 percent. Most farmers displaced by the reservoir were resettled on land within its 11,500 square kilometers of watershed. With a population density of 68 people per square kilometer, the watershed area supported 785,000 people in 1980. This number is expected to double by the year 2000.[2]

Not surprisingly, the character of watershed land use has changed dramatically. Between 1965 and 1982, more than half of the forested land in the Nam Pong Basin was converted to agricultural use, despite its poor soil and steep slopes. The watershed area, which had been largely forest, was projected to be totally deforested by 1990. Sedimentation, a direct function of the effectiveness of vegetation cover and anti-erosion practices, has increased dramatically. The average sediment flow from the Nam Pong watershed into the reservoir increased by 80 percent between 1969 and 1982. By 1990 the cumulative increase was expected to be 135 percent. During the 1980s more than 2 million tons of sediment flowed into the reservoir annually.[3]

In turn, sedimentation in the river basin reduces the effective capacity of the reservoir, cutting its potential to irrigate, generate power, control floods, and support fish. In 1980, the reservoir's expected life was reduced from 500 years to 200 years. To limit sedimentation to 3 million tons per year, the government will have to preserve the 2,500 square kilometers of national parks within the watershed. Without this maintenance, the life span of the reservoir is expected to decrease further to 157 years.[4]

The Thai government's study of the reservoir has enabled researchers to estimate benefits forgone because of watershed deforestation and inadequate erosion management. The levels of sedimentation resulting from different types of land use and erosion management, and the consequent reductions in irrigation, power, flood control, and fish catch have been calculated. Because of sedimentation, the reservoir is expected to provide only half its initial benefits by year 50.[5]

1. Sam H. Johnson III, *Physical and Economic Impacts of Sedimentation on Fishing Activities: Nam Pong, Northeast Thailand* (Urbana-Champaign: University of Illnois Press, 1984).

2. Ruandoj Srivardhana, *The Nam Pong Case Study: Some Lessons to Be Learned* (Honolulu: Environment and Policy Institute, East-West Center, 1982).

3. Johnson, *Physical and Economic Impacts of Sedimentation.*

4. Ibid.

5. John A. Dixon and Maynard M. Hufschmidt, eds., *Economic Valuation Techniques for the Environment* (Baltimore: Johns Hopkins University Press, 1986).

are being wasted on marginal investments? Why is greater effort and cost being expended when a smaller amount would generate more profits and less damage to the resource? Why are resources and by-products not recycled when recycling would generate both economic and environmental benefits? Why are local communities and tribal groups displaced and deprived of their customary rights to resources when by virtue of their physical presence and intimate knowledge they would be the most cost-effective managers of the resource? Why are unique habitats and species going extinct without compelling economic reasons to counter the irreversible loss of uniqueness, diversity, and future options?

The answers to these questions are found in the disassociation of scarcity and price, benefits and costs, rights and responsibilities, actions and consequences. This disassociation exists because of a combination of market and policy failures. The prevailing configuration of markets and policies leaves many resources outside the domain of markets, unowned, unpriced, and unaccounted for. More often than not, it subsidizes their excessive use and destruction despite their growing scarcity and rising social cost. The result is an incentive structure that induces people to maximize their profits not by being efficient and innovative but by appropriating other people's resources and shifting their own costs onto others. Common and public property resources (such as forests and fisheries) are being appropriated without compensation. The cost of growing scarcity is diluted through subsidies paid by the general taxpayer, and the ultimate cost of depletion is borne by the poor, who lack alternatives, and by future generations, whose interests are sacrificed to short-term political expediency. Preventing prices from rising in line with growing scarcities and rising social costs distorts the signals that in a well-functioning market would have brought about increased efficiency, substitution, conservation, and innovation to restore the balance between supply and demand.

Although policy and market failures are often intertwined and mutually reinforcing, for both analytical and policy reform purposes it is important to distinguish between them as clearly as possible. Policy failures or market distortions are cases of misguided government intervention in a fairly well-functioning market or unsuccessful attempts to mitigate market failures that result in worse outcomes. Market failures are institutional failures attributable partially to the nature of certain resources and partially to a failure of the government to (1) establish the fundamental conditions for markets to function efficiently (such as secure property rights and enforcement of contracts) and (2) use instruments at its disposal (such as taxation, regulation, public investment, and macroeconomic policy) to bring costs and benefits that the institutional framework fails to internalize into the domain of markets.

I will examine market and policy failures in detail in Chapters 2 and 3, respectively. I begin with market failures not because they are more important, but because they outline a potential role for government policy against which current policies can be viewed to identify areas of policy failure and policy success. If policy failure is defined as a government intervention that distorts a well-functioning market, exacerbates an existing market failure, or fails to establish the foundations for the market to function efficiently, policy success is the successful mitigation of market failures. Success consists of improvement in the allocation of resources among sectors and over time.

Before discussing market failures in detail, however, I must clarify a number of points that have often led to misunderstanding and caused some to advocate replacing markets with government institutions. First of all, as we have seen, only part of the environmental degradation in developing countries is due to genuine market failure. Much of it is due to misguided government interventions (such as tax distortions, subsidies, quotas, interest rate ceilings, and inefficient public enterprises), which distort an otherwise well-functioning market. Second, a good deal of genuine market failure, such as the failures arising from unpriced and open-access resources, insecure tenure, and to some extent uncertainty and high transaction costs, comes about because of government failure to establish the legal foundations of markets, such as secure property rights and enforcement of contracts.

Third, the mere existence of a market failure does not justify government intervention, much less abandonment of the market as a mechanism for allocating resources. Government intervention must lead to better resource allocation than the

CASE 6

Turning a Market Failure into a Policy Success:
The Dumoga-Bone National Park in Indonesia

In 1980 the Indonesian government, with assistance from the World Bank, established the Dumoga-Bone National Park in Sulawesi, Indonesia.[1] The park is unusual in that it serves the dual purpose of protecting a major irrigation area and conserving valuable wildlands.

After construction of a highway in the Dumoga Valley, the once-pristine area fell prey to rapid encroachment, especially in the wake of a government-sponsored transmigration scheme that moved thousands of new residents into the area. Increasingly, forest in the catchment area was cleared, threatening the water flow from feeder rivers and increasing the likelihood of siltation. Given this steady deterioration, the Indonesian government and the World Bank agreed the watershed area of the Dumoga Basin needed more effective management.

Their agreement led to the establishment of a 278,700 hectare national park, which has allowed scientists to make important advances in conservation biology. For example, 160 researchers from 17 countries participated in Project Wallace, which cataloged the insects of the area.

At the same time the park promotes the conservation of indigenous plant and animal species, it also insures investment in the irrigation project by guaranteeing a well-protected watershed. The two uses—an effective watershed for irrigation and conservation of wildlands—complement each other, generating benefits for both uses and society at large. The project's provisions for wildland management also serve to enhance the irrigation system by reducing sedimentation (and related maintenance costs) and helping to ensure a steady and predictable flow of water. Water fees are collected to fund both services: provision of irrigation water and wildlife preservation. For the first time, the Indonesian government explicitly recognized and assigned a value to conservation efforts as part of development.[2]

The free market could not have brought about this beneficial result, because of the prohibitive transaction costs of bringing together thousands of farmers to reach an agreement and enforcing it. In addition, the free market would have been unable to exclude free riders, who seek to gain benefits without paying the appropriate costs.

The Dumoga-Bone National Park illustrates how an irrigation project can be planned to include provisions for watershed protection that simultaneously fulfill the requirements for conservation land. These uses complement one another, while generating both economic and environmental benefits. The conversion of the watershed area into park land establishes an important linkage between biological conservation and watershed management. The project can serve as a model for other irrigation projects, showing how costs for protecting watersheds can be automatically included and justified, as a means not only of ensuring investment in irrigation but also of conserving wildlife.

---

1. At a cost of US$1.2 million, the project constituted 2 percent of a US$60 million irrigation project.

2. Jeffrey A. McNeely, "How Dams and Wildlife Can Coexist: Natural Habitats, Agriculture, and Major Water Resource Development Projects in Tropical Asia," *Journal of Conservation Biology* 1, no. 3 (October 3, 1987).

free market, and the ensuing benefits should exceed the costs of such intervention, including the costs of enforcement and side effects. Experience suggests that the most cost-effective intervention for mitigating market failures is to improve the functioning of the market by eliminating policy-induced distortions, establishing secure property rights over resources, internalizing the costs of external side effects through pricing and fiscal instruments, encouraging competition, allowing the free flow of information, and reducing uncertainty through more stable and predictable policies and politics.

It is a misconception, therefore, that the presence of market failures justifies a reduction in the role of the market in resource allocation and an increase in the role of government. To the contrary, mitigation of market failures through secure property rights, internalization of externalities, increased competition, and reduced uncertainty would enhance the role of markets in allocating resources such as water, land, fisheries, forests, and environmental services and would make it unnecessary to establish cumbersome and often inefficient public institutions for resource management and conservation. The government need only provide the initial institutional and policy reform necessary to allow the markets to function efficiently.

The first priority for developing countries is to eliminate policies that have significant environmental costs or that create perverse incentives leading to the depletion of resources and environmental degradation beyond the free-market level. Unless perverse incentives are removed, project investments aiming at improved use and conservation of resources are unlikely to succeed. If they do succeed, their impact will be unsustainable, lasting only as long as the project.

It is easiest to start by reforming policies that are detrimental to both the economy and the environment, because no budget outlays or difficult trade-offs between development and the environment are involved. If anything, eliminating policy distortions usually reduces government expenditures and may even generate additional budget revenues. This approach also has positive implications for income distribution, because many of these distortions (such as interest rate ceilings, capital subsidies, untaxed resource rents, monopolies, input subsidies, and price supports) are sources not only of inefficiency but also of inequity and perpetuation of poverty. Finally, eliminating policy distortions can be done by adjusting prices, taxes, subsidies, interest rates, and exchange rates, which is easier than introducing new instruments or developing new institutions to deal with market failures.

This is not to say that market failures need not be mitigated. Rather, the acid test of successful policy interventions is the elimination of policy-induced market distortions. Only then can market failures be seen clearly and cost-effective interventions for improving the functioning of the market be formulated and effectively implemented. There is little rationale for trying to internalize the benefits from conserving biological diversity, for example, when the wholesale conversion of tropical forests into cattle ranches or pine plantations is heavily subsidized.

CHAPTER 2

Market Failures and Environmental Degradation

Well-functioning markets are normally efficient mechanisms for allocating resources among uses and over time. To function well, markets require that certain fundamental conditions be met. For instance, property rights over all resources must be clear and secure. All scarce resources must enter active markets that price them according to supply and demand. Actions should have no significant negative side effects. Competition should prevail. Public goods should be minor exceptions. Myopia, uncertainty, and irreversible decisions should not arise. If these conditions are not met, the free market fails to allocate resources efficiently among uses and over time. It wastes too many resources today and leaves too little for the future.

Much of the mismanagement and inefficient use of natural resources and the environment can be traced to malfunctioning, distorted, or totally absent markets. Prices generated by such markets do not reflect the true social costs and benefits of resource use. Such prices convey misleading information about resource scarcity and provide inadequate incentives for management, efficient use, and conservation of natural resources.

The most important market failures affecting resource use and management are the following:

- ill-defined or nonexistent property rights

- unpriced resources and absent or thin markets

- pervasive spillover effects or linkages between sectors that are kept outside the domain of markets

- high transaction costs that discourage otherwise beneficial exchanges that would conserve resources and improve social welfare (transaction costs include the costs of information, negotiating, monitoring, and enforcement)

- public goods that cannot or should not be provided by the private sector through the market either because of an inability to exclude free riders and recover the cost of providing these goods or because excluding free riders, though technically possible, reduces social welfare

- market imperfections, particularly lack of competition in the form of local monopolies, oligopolies, and segmented markets (that is, markets fragmented by physical or policy barriers to resource mobility that prevent the equalization of returns)

- myopia, in the sense of planning horizons that are too short or discount rates that are too high, arising from poverty, impatience, and risk or uncertainty that affect individuals but not the society as a whole

- uncertainty and risk aversion, which may lead not only to high discount rates but also to unwillingness to undertake investments that are otherwise profitable but have a large variance of returns

- irreversibility (when market decisions under uncertainty lead to irreversible results, the market may fail to allocate resources prudently)

These sources of market failure are not unique either to natural resources or to developing countries. Like investment in natural resources, investment in education and human capital or science and technology can face some of these problems. Uncertainty and market imperfections permeate all sectors of the economy. No other sector, however, can claim market failures as numerous and as pervasive as the natural resource sectors. Not only are these market failures intertwined with each other, but they are also intertwined with socioeconomic and sociocultural factors such as poverty, customs, and perceptions. For historical and sociocultural reasons, many of these market failures are more pervasive and refractory in some countries than others. In this chapter, I discuss how each of these market failures contributes to the mismanagement of natural resources and the degradation of the environment.

Insecurity of Resource Ownership

A fundamental condition for the efficient operation of markets is the existence of well-defined, exclusive, secure, transferable, and enforceable property rights over all resources, goods, and services. Property rights are a precondition for efficient use, trade, investment, conservation, and management of resources. No one would economize on, pay for, invest in, or conserve a resource without an assurance that he has secure and exclusive rights over it, that he can recover his costs through use, lease, or sale, and that such rights can and will be enforced. Property rights must be *well-defined*. Otherwise they give rise to competing claims and conflicts that cause uncertainty of ownership and discourage investment, conservation, and management. The rights that accompany ownership must be fully specified, along with the restrictions that apply to owners and the corresponding rights of nonowners.

Property rights must also be *exclusive*, in the sense that others do not have similar or competing rights to the same piece of the resource. Multiple ownership, however secure, has detrimental effects on investment, conservation, and management. No single joint owner has sufficient incentive to invest in land improvements when he or she knows that all the other co-owners have a right to the benefits that accrue from this investment. Joint investment is a solution provided that the joint owners can agree on the type, scale, and financing of the investment (or conservation). The larger the number of owners and the higher the transaction or negotiation cost, the smaller the likelihood that they will reach a stable agreement. This has implications for communal management of resources, a subject I will discuss later.

Property rights need to be *secure*. If there is a challenge to ownership, risk of expropriation (without adequate compensation), or extreme political or economic uncertainty, well-defined and exclusive property rights provide little security for long-term investments such as land improvements, tree planting, and resource conservation. If long-term investments are to be encouraged, property rights must also be *indefinite*. Usufruct certificates or land titles for a specified period of time after which property rights expire do not provide the right incentives for investment and conservation. Only investments that can yield sufficient benefits within the given time framework of the property right will be undertaken. Exploitative behavior will begin as the expiration date approaches unless there is a high probability that the property right will be renewed or extended.

Property rights must be *enforceable*. Even if property rights are well defined, exclusive, and secure, they will have little effect on resource use and management if they cannot or will not be enforced. An unenforced right is effectively no right at all. This holds for both private and public property. For example, declaring forests to be public or state property, as most tropical countries have done, has done little to prevent deforestation. In fact, such declarations may have accelerated it because public ownership over vast areas has been proven unenforceable. Effective enforcement involves the discovery of violations, the apprehension of violators, and the imposition of penalties. For penalties to be effective, their expected or certainty-equivalent value (the severity of the fine multiplied by probability of apprehension) must exceed the benefit obtainable from violations. When it is difficult to enforce property rights through penalties because of sociocultural or other constraints, incentives for self-enforcement could be provided. For example, the government may rely on peer group pressure and community leadership to enforce communal and private property rights within a community that has a cohesive social organization.

Finally, property rights must be legally *transferable*, through

lease, sale, or bequest. If they are not, the incentives for investment and conservation are considerably reduced and the efficiency of resource allocation is compromised. Owners of resources who are not allowed to transfer them are discouraged
from making long-term investments because they cannot recover such investments if they change occupation or residence.
For example, a logging concessionaire has no incentive to invest in reforestation or conservation because his concession is
not transferable and his investments accumulate no equity.
Moreover, for markets to work efficiently in allocating scarce
resources between competing uses, property rights must gravitate to the highest-value use. Restrictions on transferability of
property rights are sources of inefficiency. Where there is a
justification for such restrictions, they should be imposed on
usage, not on the transfer of ownership.

For historical and sociocultural reasons, property rights
over many natural resources in developing countries are ill-
defined, insecure, and unenforceable, and in a number of cases
totally absent. Insecurely held resources can include private
agricultural land, public forest land and forest resources, irrigation systems and water resources, coastal zone and fishery
resources, and environmental resources. Resources over which
property rights do not exist and to which everyone has free
access are known as open-access or common property resources or, in layman's terms, "no-man's-land." *Common* property must be distinguished from *communal* property, which is
well-defined and enforceable.

Unpriced Resources and Thin Markets

There is no market and therefore no price for open-access resources because there is no secure and exclusive owner who
could demand such a price and in the absence of payment deny
access. Moreover, prospective buyers would be unwilling to
pay such a price as long as they have free access to the same
resource elsewhere. With no sellers and no buyers, a market
for open-access resources does not develop, and the price of
such resources remains at zero even as they become increasingly scarce. True, there are markets for natural resource

commodities such as fish, crops, and fuelwood produced from open-access resources, but the price that such commodities command reflects only the opportunity cost of labor and capital used in their production, not the opportunity cost of scarce natural resources used in their production. The implicit rent or user cost for the fishing ground, the newly opened forest land, and the forest itself is still taken to be zero, regardless of scarcity and social opportunity cost (the value to society of forgone alternative uses).

With a price of zero and no market to register scarcity, it is not surprising that natural resources are depleted at rapid rates, since demand is high and supply is low at a zero price. Conservation efforts are likely to be nonexistent at that price. In a market economy, the only gauge of scarcity is price. Price is also the mechanism through which scarcity is managed and mitigated by means of demand and supply adjustments. In the case of natural resources, supply is limited by nature and adjustments can be made only through conservation and substitution: both are costly processes that must be paid for by rising resource prices. Rising prices require working markets, and working markets require secure property rights over resources.

The absence of markets and prices is not limited to open-access resources such as fisheries and the environment. As we saw earlier, even state properties such as forests and forest lands are in effect open-access resources, because the state cannot or will not enforce its ownership. For this reason, the market in forest properties is very thin (that is, there is little competition among buyers and sellers), which is itself another market failure.

A more obvious case of an unpriced resource is irrigation water. Here, the state has made a deliberate decision to provide farmers with irrigation water free of charge or at a nominal fee. In this case, not only is the water, a scarce natural resource with a positive opportunity cost, left unpriced (or priced at zero), but so is the scarce capital invested in the irrigation systems. The consequences are many and far reaching. Water is inefficiently and wastefully used without any attempt to conserve it, even when its scarcity is obvious to the user. The state is unable to recover capital, operation, and maintenance costs, with the result that watersheds remain unprotected and the irrigation system is poorly maintained. Serious environmental problems such as sedimentation, soil salinization, and waterlogging result from watershed degradation and from overirrigation, while other potentially irrigable areas receive insufficient quantities of water to grow dry-season crops. In the final analysis, better-off farmers near the irrigation canals are indirectly subsidized by worse-off farmers who pay taxes but have little or no access to irrigation water.

It is neither technically nor politically easy to introduce water pricing, especially in societies in which water has traditionally been regarded as God-given, and therefore a free good. Yet the potential gains justify some form of water pricing in the face of increasing scarcity. The alternatives range from volumetric pricing to water rights, land taxation, contributions in kind, and self-management through water-user associations.

Pricing is at the heart of natural resource policy and management. Almost all resource problems can be traced to discrepancies between private and social valuation of resource commodities and resource stocks. In the case of irrigation water, the private cost of both the *commodity* water and the *resource* water is constant at zero, while the social cost of both is positive and rising. Similarly, the cost to the private sector of using the environment (water, land, and air) for waste disposal is zero, while the cost to the society is positive and rising. Rapid deforestation and slow reforestation, even in securely owned forest land, is partly the consequence of the failure of the market to price forest products to capture the effects on watersheds, wildlife, and other nonmarketed services of the forest.

In general, overexploitation, inefficient use, inadequate conservation, and lack of investment in regeneration of natural resources arise from the failure of either the market or the government to price natural resources according their social scarcity. The keys to optimal pricing of natural resources are, first, to identify and measure correctly the external social costs (the spillover effects damaging other activities that are ignored in private benefit-cost calculations) and the intertemporal user costs (the effects of current resource use on future resource availability) of resource exploitation; and, second, to internalize these costs or charge them to the current generation of consumers through appropriate pricing or taxation.

Spillover Effects or Externalities

A major factor that drives a wedge between private and social valuation of resources and leads to inefficient pricing is the presence of external costs or spillover effects known as externalities. An externality is an effect of one firm's or individual's actions on other firms or individuals who are not parties in those actions. Externalities may be positive or negative. A positive externality, for example, is the benefit that upstream forest owners provide to downstream farmers in the form of a steady water supply made possible by a forested watershed. It is to the society's (and the farmer's) benefit that more of such positive externalities are provided, but since the forest owners receive no payment for their watershed service, they have no incentive to provide more of this service by logging less and planting more. The result is that more logging and less planting than is socially optimal takes place.

From another perspective, logging has negative externalities for downstream activities such as farming, irrigation, transport, and industry in the form of flooding, sedimentation, and irregular water supply. These are real costs to downstream activities and to the society as a whole, but not to upstream loggers or shifting cultivators, who have no cause or incentive to consider them because they do not affect the profitability of logging or shifting cultivation. In fact, taking such costs into account voluntarily amounts to a conscious decision to lower one's profit and price oneself out of the market. Unless every logger and every shifting cultivator takes such external costs into account, those who do are certain to lose to competitors who do not. This is precisely why government intervention is necessary to establish and enforce similar standards and incentives or disincentives for all competitors.

Another example of a negative externality is the damage that an upstream rice farmer's use of pesticides causes to a downstream fish farmer who uses the same water source. Not only the fish farmer, but also society as a whole would be better off if less of this negative externality were produced. Again, however, there is no incentive for the upstream farmer to take the downstream farmer's interest into account. The government may react to this problem by banning the use of pesticides altogether. This action, however, may reduce social welfare if the loss from rice production outweighs the gain from fish production (and if no other environmental effects are involved). The ideal solution would be to reduce pesticide use to exactly the level where the combined value of rice and fish is maximized. This level occurs when the marginal benefit from pesticide use equals its marginal cost, where this cost is understood to include both the production cost of the pesticide and its environmental cost (that is, its effect on fish production).[1] This solution is possible if the price of pesticide that the rice farmer pays includes a surcharge above the production cost to account for the pesticide's environmental cost or if the same decision maker owns both the rice farm and the fish farm.

Will a free market produce either of these outcomes? The answer is no, except under very special circumstances. Environmental costs are outside the domain of markets, because these costs arise from a technological rather than a market interdependence between economic activities. One fundamental premise of an efficiently functioning market is that economic units interact only through their effect on prices; technological interdependence is ruled out. The market, however, can stretch itself to account for a technological interdependence if it is a private externality. If there is only one rice farmer and one fish farmer, one of the two (or both) will recognize that one could buy off the other, combine the two operations, and end up with a profit because, as we have seen, combined profits exceed the sum of individual profits. Alternatively, the fish farmer may offer to "bribe" the rice farmer to reduce the use of the pesticide if the latter has the right to pollute. Or, if the fish farmer has the right to clean water, the rice farmer may offer to bribe him to accept more water pollution. In either case the result will be an improvement in social welfare by means of internalization of the externality through the free market.

As the number of polluters and affected parties (say, rice and fish farmers, or upstream loggers and downstream farmers) increases, however, the market becomes less and less able to internalize externalities. First, the damage is spread over so many decision makers that it is not perceived as important enough by any individual decision maker to induce action, even though its aggregate effect might be enormous. Second, it is difficult to unscramble cause and effect or who damages whom and by how much. Third, another market failure comes into play: as the number of parties involved rises, so do information and transaction costs. Bringing people together and obtaining an agreement becomes prohibitively expensive. A smooth functioning of markets assumes that information and transaction costs are zero or insignificant. In the case of public externalities, that is, spillovers involving a large number of polluters and affected parties, transaction costs may be so high that they will eat up all benefits from their internalization. Government intervention is justified provided that the government can bring about a more cost-effective internalization of externalities than the market. For example, a surcharge on the price of pesticides or wood to reflect the environmental costs of pesticide use and logging is likely to generate net social benefits if appropriately set and administered.

Environmental pollution is a classic case of a public externality. It originates from a variety of sources including discharges of domestic wastewater, community solid wastes, industrial waste effluents, and wastes from agricultural activities such as runoff of excess pesticides and fertilizers. It affects a variety of economic activities including industry, fisheries, tourism, and urban development, as well as the general quality of life. Thus, excessive environmental pollution constitutes both a misuse of an unpriced or open-access resource and a negative externality on sectors and individuals who may or may not be parties to the pollution-generating activity. This is so because the environment serves as both the *recipient* of the residuals of economic activity and the *medium* that transmits offsite effects to second and third parties. Externalities created by economic activity in one area proliferate and become widespread through the environment.

To sum up, the market mechanism may work out a solution as long as the externality is private or at least concentrated and important enough for the benefits of internalization to be apparent to all parties involved. Alternatively, at least one of the parties involved may have such a large stake as to be induced to act even though other beneficiaries will be getting a free ride. When the external effects are too widely spread, as is usually the case, the correction of the externality is a public good. In such a case, the market does not function effectively, and government intervention might be necessary if the externality is worth rectifying. Not all externalities are worth correcting, and few, if any, are worth eliminating entirely. The guiding principle should be that the gains in social welfare from correcting an externality should outweigh the costs of the intervention, including any distortions in the rest of the economy that such an intervention might introduce.

It may be useful at this point to relate externalities to open-access property and insecurity of ownership. Open-access property creates externalities, and externalities create insecurity of ownership. Users impose externalities on each other, which they ignore to everyone's detriment. The larger the catch of one fisherman, the higher the fishing cost of all other fishermen. Since this cost is ignored, everyone's catch and costs are higher than necessary, leading to economic and biological overfishing and ultimately to social loss. Similarly, pervasive externalities may lead to insecurity of ownership with the same devastating overexploitation as occurs under open access. A farmer with a secure and exclusive title to a piece of land subject to increasing erosion or flooding caused by upstream deforestation may decide to mine rather than farm his land before it is washed away, an outcome identical to that of open-access property.

The failure of the market to price externalities or to account for environmental costs is a major reason for the undervaluation of natural resources or for the discrepancy between the private and social benefits and costs of exploiting them. The market fails to deal with externalities for two related reasons, themselves major market failures. Correction of public externalities involves prohibitively high transaction costs and is itself a public good. I now turn to these two market failures.

Transaction Costs

Markets emerge to make possible beneficial exchanges or trade between parties with different resource endowments and different preferences. Establishing and operating markets, however, is not costless. Transaction costs—the costs of information, coordination, bargaining, and enforcement of contracts—are involved. Usually such costs are trivial compared with the benefits from trade that such markets make possible. Markets fail to emerge, however, if there are very high set-up costs, if the costs per unit transacted exceed the difference between the supply and demand price, or if there are only a small number of buyers and sellers. The absence of well-defined property rights prevents markets from emerging, but well-defined property rights do not bring markets into existence if the coordination and marketing costs, necessary for the commodity in question to be traded voluntarily, are very high. Even if markets appear, they tend to be thin and inactive. The absence or paucity of futures markets and the high cost of rural credit are usually attributed to high transaction costs.

Similarly, there are costs to establishing and enforcing property rights. If such transaction costs are high relative to the benefits of secure and exclusive ownership, property rights and the related markets will fail to emerge. For example, the costs of parceling out the sea to individual fishermen and enforcing property rights over a mobile resource are prohibitively high. Analogous is the case of externalities. There are costs related to identifying the afflicted and generating parties and to negotiating a mutually agreeable solution. The more parties involved, the less likely that a bargaining solution will be arrived at voluntarily because the transaction cost tends to exceed the benefits from internalizing the externality. The government, however, either through its collective or coercive power, may be able to internalize externalities at a lower transaction cost than the free market. According to Joseph Stiglitz, "The internalization of externalities or the reduction of related welfare losses could be thought of as a rationale for the existence of governments."[2]

Public Goods

When several originators and recipients are involved, externalities such as water and air pollution may be considered public "bads," and their correction a public good. In fact, a public good may be thought of as an extreme case of a good that has only externalities; that is, no part of it is private to any individual. Each individual's consumption of such a good depends on the total quantity of the good supplied in the economy. Unlike the case with private goods, the consumption of a public good by an individual does not diminish its availability to other individuals. Although the production of public goods involves an opportunity cost in terms of forgone quantities of private or other public goods, a zero opportunity cost is associated with its consumption.

A public good is characterized by jointness in supply, in that to produce the good for one consumer it is necessary to produce it for all consumers. In many cases, individuals cannot be excluded from the enjoyment of a public good whether they pay for it or not (for example, national defense). Even if exclusion is possible (for instance, from a bridge across a river), to do so violates Pareto optimality, which requires that no opportunity of making one person better off without making anyone else worse off is left unused. Because nobody can or should be excluded from the benefits of a public good, consumers will not freely pay for it; hence, no firm would be able to cover its production cost though the market. The free market will therefore fail to supply a public good, even though the good would contribute to social welfare. Thus, a free market will lead to underproduction of public goods and overproduction of private goods.

Because individual consumers cannot adjust the amount of the public good they consume, a market for it cannot exist. If a semblance of such a market does exist, it does not provide the public good in sufficient quantities. This situation provides a rationale for many government activities aimed at providing public goods. For the government to provide a public good, it must know each individual's marginal rate of substitution between the public and private goods, which would determine the optimal level of the public good and perhaps each individual's share of the cost. Consumers, however, may not reveal their true preferences for fear they will be taxed on the basis of their willingness to pay. Public goods are therefore usually produced or contracted out by public agencies on the basis of collective decisions and financed from general taxation. Thus, although consumers consume the same amount of the public good (such as defense or clean air), they pay different "prices," whereas in the case of a private good, such as food or clothing of a given quality, consumers pay the same price but consume different quantities of the good. In other words, public goods are provided in certain quantities and are paid from taxes based on a notion of "ability to pay" rather than the quantity of the good consumed. Private goods, in contrast, are provided at certain prices reflecting the long-run production costs, and consumers purchase the quantity each wants according to his or her income and preferences or tastes.

The environment involves many public goods, ranging from environmental quality and watershed protection to ecological balance and biological diversity. In addition, the organizational services necessary to internalize the externality can be seen as public goods. Moreover, many externalities involve the provision of public goods such as clean air, clean water, watershed protection, and biological diversity. Since it is very costly (and often detrimental to social welfare) to exclude anyone who does not pay from enjoying the benefits from public goods, such goods cannot (and should not) be provided by the market. They can be best provided by the government and financed from general taxation. In some cases, however, public goods could be provided by nongovernmental organizations (NGOs) through voluntary contributions by members or supplied by the private sector under contract with the government.

Geographically, public goods range in scope from local and regional to national and global. For example, biological diversity is a global public good since it is not possible or desirable to exclude other nations from benefiting from its conservation. Therefore, it is unreasonable to expect such a good to be provided in sufficient quantity by an individual country in a free market.

Certain goods are referred to as "publicly provided private goods" because of the high marginal cost associated with supplying additional individuals. Such goods are supplied by the public sector because of their high set-up costs and the high transaction costs of operating a market for these goods. When private goods are freely provided, they are overconsumed. Since consumers do not pay for the good, they demand and use it until the marginal benefit they receive from the good is zero, although the marginal cost to the society is positive and often substantial. The social loss from overconsumption is the difference between the individual's willingness to pay and the marginal supply cost.[3]

A classic example of a publicly provided private good is irrigation water, whose overconsumption involves a double loss: a direct welfare loss from excessive consumption and an indirect loss from waterlogging resulting from overconsumption. There is a need for a rationing system to control consumption. Three possible rationing devices are (1) uniform provision, (2) queuing, and (3) user charges. The problem with uniform provision is that all consumers get the same amount regardless of their individual needs and desires. The problem with queuing is that it requires payment in the form of waiting time and rewards those whose opportunity cost is lowest. User charges are particularly suited to publicly provided private goods because users can be charged the marginal cost of providing the good, which is often substantial though not sufficient to cover the total cost of the public good. User charges result in both more efficient use and partial recovery of costs. This is particularly relevant to irrigation water pricing. According to Warren C. Baum and Stokes M. Tolbert,

> True efficiency pricing requires accurate measurement of supplies by metering the volume of water delivered to individual users. . . . Although true efficiency pricing may not be attainable, even a nominal charge for irrigation water would provide an incentive to use it more efficiently.[4]

These complications notwithstanding, the pervasive shortage of public funds and the large income benefits derived from participants in irrigation schemes suggest that substantial cost recovery should be the goal in many instances. Most governments, however, have not attained anything like a full cost recovery from public irrigation schemes (see Table 2). A rule of thumb followed by some governments is to absorb the capital costs but to set water charges and benefit taxes at a level that in the aggregate will allow recovery of the operation and maintenance costs, including repairs.

I should note that even when there is a marginal cost

TABLE 2

Cost Recovery in Public Irrigation Systems in Selected
Developing Countries

Country	Annual revenues (US$/hectare)	Total costs (US$/hectare)	Total costs as % of revenues	Annual charges as % of economic benefits to farmers
Indonesia	25.90	191.00	735	8
Korea	192.00	1,057.00	550	26
Nepal	9.10	126.00	1,388	5
Thailand	8.31	151.00	1,818	9
Philippines	16.85	75.00	443	10

SOURCE: Robert Repetto, "Economic Policy Reform for Natural Resource Conservation," Environment Working Paper (Washington, D.C.: World Bank, May 1988).

associated with each individual using a good, if the transaction costs of collecting user charges are very high, it may be more efficient for the government to provide the good and finance it from general taxation. Raising revenues through taxes, however, such as the income tax, may introduce distortions, such as disincentives for work and investment, that raise the effective amount of private goods that individuals must give up to obtain an additional unit of the public good above the nominal cost.

Uncompetitive Markets

Even when markets do exist and are active, market failures may occur in the form of insufficient competition. For markets to be efficient there should be a large number of buyers and sellers of a more or less homogeneous commodity, or at least a lack of barriers to entry and a large number of potential entrants as insurance against monopolistic practices by existing firms. In reality, however, economies are ridden with monopolistic elements.

A market is imperfectly competitive if the actions of one or a few sellers or buyers have a perceptible influence on the price. Market imperfections may arise for a variety of reasons. A major source of monopolistic tendencies, affecting some resource-related sectors such as water and energy supply, is their decreasing industry cost feature. Because of the indivisibility of the necessary investment, the average cost of the service falls continuously as more and more customers are served until the whole market is dominated by a single firm (known as a natural monopoly). To prevent monopolistic practices, a government monopoly may be established, as is often the case with utilities and the postal service.

Other causes of limited competition are institutional, legal, or political barriers to entry into certain professions or industries; high information costs; and the limited size of the market. The latter is a common problem in developing countries and may result in oligopolies because a few firms by themselves can easily supply the entire market.

A common monopolistic practice is to withhold supplies in order to raise prices. The monopolist's price is too high and his output too low for social optimality, which requires marginal cost pricing rather than the monopolist's average cost pricing. But monopoly is not altogether bad for conservation. The monopolist may approximate the socially optimal rate of resource extraction for the wrong reason. Even though a monopolist is likely to ignore the environmental cost of his activities, his fear of depressing the price turns him into a conservationist. This is not to imply that a monopoly is a solution to resource depletion: replacing one market failure with another does not usually improve welfare.

One market whose imperfections are likely to have more pronounced effects on natural resources than on the other sectors of the economy is the capital market. Ideally, economic activities and business ventures that promise to yield a net return higher than the going interest rate should be able to obtain funds for investment because they expect to earn enough to pay the cost of borrowed capital and still earn a profit. In reality, this does not always happen. Unless farmers already have sufficient property or capital assets to use as collateral and unless they understand and are able to meet rigid repayment requirements, they cannot obtain institutional credit at the going rate of interest. Most farmers, being either subsistence or small-scale commercial farmers, have access only to noninstitutional credit that comes with high interest rates and, more often than not, debilitating preemptive marketing arrangements. This means that even if a project is profitable at the institutional rate of interest (say 15 percent), it may be unprofitable at the much higher cost of informal credit (usually above 50 percent). Thus, unless the government makes collateral-free credit available to small farmers at the institutional rate of interest, many privately and socially worthwhile projects will not be undertaken.

There are at least two reasons why farmers and other rural dwellers have no access to institutional credit. First, many farmers have no secure land title to use as collateral; semi-secure titles are not accepted for the long-term institutional credit required for long-term investments such as land improvement and tree planting. Second, interest rate ceilings ostensibly intended to help rural borrowers result in the drying up of rural credit because banks are unwilling to lend at a loss (rural credit involves higher transaction costs than urban credit), leaving the far more costly informal credit as the only recourse for rural borrowers. Since informal credit is both costly and short-term, rural investments are biased against natural resource activities such as tree planting and soil conservation.

Myopic Planning Horizons and High Discount Rates

Natural resource conservation and sustainable development ultimately involve sacrificing present consumption for the promise of future benefits. Because people tend to prefer immediate over future benefits, such an exchange appears unattractive unless one dollar of sacrifice today yields more than one dollar of benefits tomorrow. Future benefits are therefore discounted, and the more heavily they are discounted the less attractive they are. A high rate of discount may discourage conservation altogether. Colin Clark has shown that a sufficiently high market rate of interest combined with a low natural growth rate of a species may lead to its extinction.[5] If the market rate of interest accurately reflects the society's rate of time preference, such extinction should not be worrisome (except for another market failure that results from the combination of irreversibility and uncertainty, which will be discussed later). Here I am concerned with the possibility that the market rate of interest (the discount rate) fails to reflect the society's true rate of time preference. A combination of poverty, impatience, and risk, which either does not apply or applies to a smaller degree to the society as a whole than to individuals, drives a wedge between the private and social discount rate. Because of its continuity and risk-pooling capacity, a society tends to be less myopic than its individual members.

Environmental and market uncertainties coupled with a short and uncertain life span lead people to adopt myopic time horizons and discount rates, which result in short-sighted decisions in pursuit of survival or quick profits at the expense of long-term sustainable benefits. At subsistence levels of living, when people's very survival is at stake, a hand-to-mouth economy prevails in which the future is infinitely discounted. The results of such myopia are overexploitation of natural resources and underinvestment in their conservation and regeneration, which ultimately lead to their depletion. The high cost of rural credit from informal sources, in the absence of institutional credit, also leads to high rates of discount. Conservation projects that would have been profitable at interest rates of 10 or 15 percent are not profitable at the 50 or even 100 percent rates charged by informal credit sources.[6] Again, there is scope for government intervention to induce longer time horizons and lower discount rates (through increased savings), to regulate resource extraction, and to invest in the conservation and regeneration of resources according to the society's true time preference.

There is a clear relationship between this market failure and the ones discussed earlier. Exploitation of common property[7] or open-access resources is equivalent to the use of an infinite discount rate. That is, future benefits sacrificed by current resource use are infinitely discounted, effectively assigned a zero value by the common "owners," regardless of their value to society. This is understandable since, under open access, no one is assured of the benefits of his investments and conservation efforts since others have free access to the same resource. Under open access, there is no future: common property is transformed into private property through prompt capture and use. From the individual's point of view, conservation is meaningless and irrational under open-access conditions.

Public externalities or environmental costs and benefits are also infinitely discounted by an unregulated market, regardless of whether they occur at present or in the future. Discounting is related as well to the underpricing of resources and high transaction costs that discourage the establishment of futures markets.

Uncertainty and Risk Aversion

Natural resource management and conservation is about the future, a future that is beset with uncertainties and risks. A situation involves uncertainty if more than one outcome is (or is perceived to be) possible from any given action. Two types of uncertainty can be distinguished: (1) environmental uncertainty arising from factors beyond the control of a decision maker (say, a farmer), such as weather, epidemic disease, and technological discoveries; and (2) market uncertainty arising from a market failure to provide information (prices) required for decisions affecting the future. The longer the time horizon, the further into the future forecasts need to be made and the greater the uncertainties involved.

A distinction should be made between uncertainty and risk. A situation is said to involve uncertainty if no objective probability for each of the many possible outcomes can be attached. In contrast, risk is a situation where the general level of probability of each outcome can be inferred, although known probabilities cannot be precisely assigned. In everyday terms, a situation is said to be risky if one of the outcomes involves losses to the decision maker. Thus, the risk of loss to a firm or a farm may be defined as the probability that profits will be less than zero or that returns will fall below some "disaster level" of income.

Risks can be reduced through diversification of activities with potentially negative outcomes. Risks in one activity can also be reduced by pooling them with risks from other independent activities. When many decision makers face a given type of risk that is independent of their actions, risk-pooling or insurance markets have often emerged. Individuals transfer their risks to an insurance company in exchange for paying an insurance premium, which in a perfect insurance market would equal the administrative costs of the company plus the cost of any remaining risk.

Not all risks are insurable. Insurance markets fail to appear when the outcome is not external to the policyholder, when the risk affects all policyholders in a similar way, or when the probabilities of the various outcomes are difficult to assess. For example, a farm cannot insure itself against the risk of losses because profitability is as much a function of the farmer's actions as it is of environmental uncertainty (such as weather). Similarly, a fish farm cannot insure itself against the risk of an epidemic, because such risk would affect all farms in a similar way, which reduces the benefits from risk pooling.

Risks may be objective or subjective. Objective risks are calculated on the basis of the probability of occurrence of the adverse outcome. Attitudes toward risk differ among individuals based on sociocultural and economic factors. In general, risk aversion tends to be stronger among lower socioeconomic groups because survival is at stake.

While uncertainty affects all sectors of the economy, natural resource sectors are more seriously affected for a variety of reasons. First, there are more uncertainties about ownership of and access to natural resources. Second, there are more potential spillovers from other activities. Third, natural resource investments such as tree planting tend to have much longer gestation periods than investments in agriculture or industry, and the longer the gestation period the more the uncertainties and risks involved. Fourth, natural resource commodity prices are subject to more violent fluctuations than other commodities and thus they are difficult to forecast. Last, most resource commodities are under the constant threat of being replaced by cheaper substitutes developed by continuous but unpredictable technological change.

Uncertainty about the future should make people more conservative in natural resource exploitation. Therefore it should work in favor of conservation of at least those resources that are least likely to be replaced by technology, such as biological diversity. After all, one reason people save is to provide themselves with a cushion against future uncertainty. Insecurity of tenure and pervasive externalities, however, create uncertainty about the benefits of conservation compared with the benefits of current exploitation. For the individual, it makes good economic sense to cut down the forest and mine the land to generate income, which he can then consume or invest in more secure assets. From society's point of view, it makes more sense to preserve the long-term productivity of the resource base both as a source of income in perpetuity and as insurance against uncertainty. Liquidating the resource base in the face of uncertainty on the basis of short-term economics makes little sense, however, if such an action is also irreversible.

Irreversibility

Market decisions about the future (such as the choice between consumption and investment) are made with the best available, yet incomplete, information about future developments, on the assumption that such decisions can be reversed if they prove unwise in the light of new information. This assumption of reversibility does not hold in many decisions involving natural resources. Consider the choice between preserving a tropical rain forest with some unique features and developing the site for logging and mining concessions. If the social benefits from development exceed the social benefits from conservation even marginally, the decision maker should choose logging and mining, except for the fact that conservation is reversible, while logging and mining are not. Choosing logging and mining forecloses his options; if he or future generations were to have a change of mind there would be no way to reproduce the uniqueness and authenticity of the original tropical forests and any species that became extinct. In contrast, choosing conservation preserves his option to reverse his decision. Clearly, there is a social value or shadow price for the preservation of options, though it is difficult to estimate. There are reasons, however, to favor a high value. On the one hand, technical change is asymmetric: it expands our ability to produce ordinary goods, the products of development, but it does little to improve our ability to produce natural environments, the products of conservation. On the other hand, consumer preferences tend to shift in favor of environmental services relative to ordinary goods. In conclusion, according to John Krutilla and Anthony Fisher, when economic decisions have uncertain and irreversible effects, there is a value to keeping the option of avoiding those effects open.[8]

CHAPTER 3

Policy Failures and Environmental Degradation

The tendency of free markets to fail in the allocation and efficient use of natural resources and the environment opens an opportunity and provides a rationale for government intervention. Market failure by itself, however, is a necessary but not a sufficient condition for intervention. To be truly worthwhile, a government intervention must meet two other conditions. First, the intervention must outperform the market or improve its function. Second, the benefits from such intervention must exceed the costs of planning, implementation, and enforcement, as well as any indirect and unintended costs of distortions introduced to other sectors of the economy by such intervention.

Ideally, government intervention aims at correcting or at least mitigating market failures through taxation, regulation, private incentives, public projects, macroeconomic management, and institutional reform. For example, if the market fails to allocate land to its best possible use because of insecurity of land ownership, government intervention ought to be the issuance of secure land titles through cadastral surveys and land registration, provided the ensuing benefits exceed the costs. If, on the other hand, the market fails to allocate land to its best possible use because of severe flooding due to upstream deforestation, the government ought to explore the costs and benefits of taxation on upstream logging or downstream agriculture and the use of the proceeds to subsidize upstream reforestation. If economic analysis that considers all costs and benefits involved leads to the conclusion that such an intervention can make both upstream loggers (or shifting cultivators) and downstream farmers better off, and no one else worse off (including the government treasury), it would be a policy failure not to act. Such an intervention is not a distortion, but a mitigation or correction of a distortion introduced by a failing market.[1]

In practice, however, government policies tend to introduce additional distortions in the market for natural resources rather than correct existing ones. The reasons are many and varied. First, correction of market failure is rarely the sole or even the primary objective of government intervention. Other objectives such as national security, social equity, macroeconomic management, and political expediency may dominate. Second, government intervention often has unintended consequences and unforeseen or underestimated side effects. Third, policies such as subsidies and protection against imports or competition often outlive their usefulness because they become capitalized into people's expectations and property values, creating vested interests that make their removal politically difficult. Fourth, policy interventions tend to accumulate and interact with each other in subtle but profound ways to distort private incentives away from socially beneficial activities. Finally, policies that are seemingly unrelated to natural resources and the environment may have more pronounced effects on the environment than environmental and resource policies. For example, capital subsidies, tax and tariff exemptions for equipment, and minimum wage laws that displace labor lead to increased pressures on forest, marginal lands, coastal areas, and urban slums. For example, in Ghana a grossly overvalued exchange rate resulting from macroeconomic mismanagement has nullified what otherwise was an efficient forest policy, accelerated deforestation by exacerbating poverty, and foiled reforestation by making reforestation incentives irrelevant (see Case 7 on page 60).

Thus, environmental degradation results not only from

overreliance on a free market that fails to function efficiently (market failure), but also from government policies that intentionally or unwittingly distort incentives in favor of overexploitation and against conservation of valuable and scarce resources (policy failure).

Policy failures may be classified into four basic types. One type involves distortions of otherwise well-functioning markets through taxes, subsidies, quotas, regulations, inefficient state enterprises, and public projects with a low economic return and a high environmental impact. This is a case of fixing what is not broken.

A second type is the failure to consider and internalize any significant environmental side effects of otherwise warranted policy interventions. For example, fertilizer subsidies may have a useful role to play in encouraging farmers to adopt new high-yielding crop varieties. In selecting the types of fertilizers to subsidize and in setting the level and duration of the subsidy, however, policy makers should factor in the effects on farmers' choices of other inputs (such as manure, soil conservation, weeding, and irrigation) and on long-term productivity. Moreover, the potential offsite damage from contamination and eutrophication of water resources from overuse and runoff should be considered and mitigated by setting a lower subsidy for a shorter period and promoting soil conservation, organic fertilizers, and integrated pest management (IPM). For example, in its drive for rice self-sufficiency, Indonesia provided generous subsidies for a variety of pesticides. These subsidies led to overuse, which, in turn, decimated the predators of the brown planthopper, an insect that threatened the country's self-sufficiency in rice. In a dramatic move, the government turned what was threatening to be a policy failure into a policy success by abolishing the subsidy and promoting the lower-cost strategy of IPM (see Case 8 on page 64). Many other countries, however, continue to subsidize pesticides very heavily (see Figure 1).

A third type of policy failure is government intervention that aims to correct or mitigate a market failure but ends up generating a worse outcome than a free and failing market would have produced. It must be recognized that market failure does not mandate government intervention. It merely

CASE 7

Policy Failure: Deforestation in Ghana

In 1900 more than one-third of Ghana was covered with natural forest. At present, little remains. Since the mid-1960s, the immediate causes of this deforestation have primarily been shifting cultivation of crops and the collection of fuelwood, with logging and treecropping playing a marginal role. Underlying these causes is the increasing rural and urban poverty that has resulted from the country's misguided macroeconomic policies.[1]

Ghana has experienced such extreme rates of deforestation that in 1980 only 7 percent of the country remained forested. Poverty has resulted in the halving of forested area over the past twenty-five years, as rural families, lacking other alternatives, turned to shifting cultivation for their energy needs. By 1980 nearly 40 percent of the country's land was being used for shifting cultivation. Poverty rates jumped in 1970, a condition reflected in a rapid growth in fuelwood consumption in the 1970s. By 1983 Ghana's rate of fuelwood use, 906 cubic meters per capita, ranked among the highest in the world.

The increasing poverty can be attributed to the country's macroeconomic policies. At its independence in 1957, Ghana had one of the wealthiest and most highly educated populations in sub-Saharan Africa. Between 1965 and 1983, the country's real per capita growth rate of gross national product was –2.1 percent, 5.6 percentage points lower than the average for other oil-importing middle-income developing countries. Economists concur in attributing this decline to the government's agricultural, industrial, and trade policies.

Logging and conversion to treecropping, however, have dwindled as these same policies, in particular the highly overvalued exchange rate, have undermined export profitability and limited the foreign exchange available for necessary inputs. Between 1970 and 1985, the volume of the country's industrial logging was one-tenth that of its fuelwood harvesting. Ghana's cocoa exports had represented almost one-third of the world market in the early 1960s but dropped to less than 15 percent by 1982.

To the extent that logging has been profitable, Ghana's per tree, species-specific royalty system should have resulted in efficient logging with high utilization rates for secondary species and smaller sizes of trees. By collecting royalties according to number of trees rather than the volume of timber cut, the system should have encouraged the cutting of oversized trees rather than young trees, which would have ensured canopy openings for remaining saplings. This incentive, however, has been irrelevant in the context of an exchange rate so overvalued that real fees for logging have been negligible. While officially high, royalty rates have been the lowest in the world at the black market exchange rate, making Ghanaian forest wood essentially a free good.

Similarly, the exchange rate has foiled reforestation efforts by eroding the value of revenue sources. Before 1976 the reforestation charge on loggers was equal to only US$0.02 per hectare at the black market exchange rate. After 1986 it was still less than US$0.05 per hectare. The Forestry Department's recent reforestation budget has been equivalent to approximately US$125,000 per year at the black market rate.

---

1. Material for this case comes from Malcolm Gillis, "West Africa: Resource Management Policies and the Tropical Forest," in Robert Repetto and Malcolm Gillis, eds., *Public Policies and the Misuse of Forest Resources* (New York: Cambridge University Press, 1988).

FIGURE 1

Estimated Average Rate of Pesticide Subsidies in Selected
Developing Countries

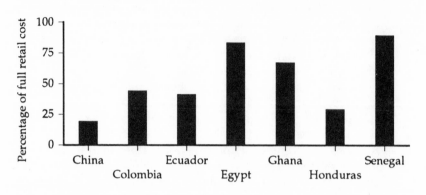

SOURCE: Robert Repetto, "Economic Policy Reform for Natural Resource Conservation," Environment Working Paper (Washington, D.C.: World Bank, May 1988).

suggests the possibility that such intervention might prove beneficial. In some cases, doing nothing might be the best policy if intervening would make matters worse. In most cases, however, the problem is not that no action is indicated, but that the wrong action is being taken. For example, if the free market fails to contain deforestation because the forests are open-access resources and the negative externalities of deforestation are not internalized (that is, paid for by the parties responsible), a logging ban is unlikely to be effective. First, higher prices are likely to stimulate illegal logging, and second, concessionaires may log illegally to recover sunk costs, or they may abandon their concessions to encroachers and slash-and-burn cultivators, as Thailand is discovering following the January 1989 logging ban in response to the catastrophic landslides of November 1988 (see Case 9 on page 68).

The last type of policy failure is a lack of intervention in failing markets when such intervention is clearly needed to improve the functioning of the market and could be made at costs fully justified by the expected benefits. For example, it would have been a policy failure for the government of Thailand not to issue secure land titles to its farmers, when it was established that the cost of titling was only a small percentage (less than 10 percent) of the potential benefits (see Case 10 on page 72). By intervening in the land market to establish secure property rights, a precondition for well-functioning markets, the government has turned a market failure into a policy success. In contrast, the issuance of twenty-five-year usufruct or stewardship rights to squatters on public lands in Thailand and the Philippines is a half-measure that does not go to the root of the problem. It is likely to stimulate continued encroachment without significantly improving farmers' security of ownership, access to credit, and incentives to invest. Such half-measures risk turning a market failure into a policy failure of possibly greater dimensions.

To sum up, policy failures include both the failure to intervene when necessary and beneficial and the failure to refrain from intervention when unnecessary and detrimental. The policy failures that lead to environmental degradation range from poorly designed public projects that fail to account for their environmental effects to structural adjustment programs that fail to internalize or at least cushion their environmental repercussions. Policy failures are not the exclusive domain of governments. Development assistance agencies, through their project and program lending and policy dialogue, may introduce or exacerbate a policy failure. For example, liberalization as part of a structural or sectoral adjustment loan, in the absence of secure property rights and other legal foundations of markets, may simply transform a policy failure into a market failure, an outcome not uncommon with African liberalization programs.

Another way of analyzing policy failures is to divide them into project-related failures, sectoral policy failures, and macroeconomic policy failures. Project-related policy failures occur especially when projects are selected on the basis of financial appraisal or narrow economic analysis that does not internalize environmental externalities. Sectoral policy failures are policies that ignore long-term costs and intersectoral linkages and spillovers. Sectoral policies may in turn be divided into agricultural and industrial policies or even more narrowly into land policy, water resource policy, forest policy, fisheries policy, urban development policy, industrial location policy, and

---

CASE 8

Policy Success:
Removal of Pesticide Subsidies in Indonesia

Until 1985 the Indonesian government subsidized pesticides at 82 percent of the retail price, at an annual cost of US$128 million.[1] These heavy subsidies stimulated a 76 percent increase in pesticide use by Indonesian farmers between 1976 and 1985, with devastating results. The widespread use of the pesticide Sevin wiped out the natural predators of the brown planthopper, and millions of tons of rice were lost to a pest that had not even been considered a threat in the early 1970s.[2] In 1976 alone, 364,500 tons of rice, valued at US$100 million, were lost.[3]

Overuse of pesticides often leads to the evolution of resistant strains of some pests, while wiping out natural predators that help control pests. Excessive pesticide use has in fact been linked to a *reduction* in productivity. In northern Sumatra, the density of the brown planthopper population rose directly with the number of pesticide applications.[4] Meanwhile, research has shown that untreated fields had 75 percent fewer planthoppers and higher yields.[5]

Like other market failures, subsidies obstruct important market signals that would prevent farmers from overusing pesticides. Because they pay artificially low prices for pesticides, farmers tend to use more than the economic optimum, the point at which the true cost of pesticide use begins to exceed the benefit of using more pesticide. As a result, farmers continue to use pesticides, perhaps as a substitute for other inputs such as weeding, despite increasing damage to crops and the environment. In Indonesia, insecticides were generously applied four to five times a season over millions of hectares of rice fields, regardless of the needs of individual fields.[6]

By late 1985, 70 percent of Java's rice crop was threatened, and numerous economic studies showed negative returns to heavy insecticide use. A policy designed to promote rice self-sufficiency had jeopardized the crop yields it was intended to bolster. The brown planthopper was inflicting increasingly severe damage on supposedly resistant varieties of rice. Describing the damage, the Food and

Agriculture Organization (FAO) reported, "Even extremely high dosages of insecticides could not stop these outbreaks. To the contrary, they seemed to make things worse."[7]

In November 1986 President Suharto issued a decree banning fifty-seven brands of pesticide, twenty of which were heavily subsidized by the government. The same decree established a national pest control strategy for rice called integrated pest management (IPM), which involved using the pests' natural predators. Three planting seasons after the decree, FAO reported a 90 percent reduction in pesticide use. Moreover, average yields rose from 6.1 tons per hectare to 7.4 tons.

In October 1988 the Indonesian government cut pesticide subsidies from 55 percent to 40 percent of retail prices. Shortly after, in December, the government opted to eliminate pesticide subsidies altogether. Although fiscal concerns played an important role, policy makers also hoped the cuts would cause farmers to use pesticides more efficiently.[8] The government also issued provisions for raising the floor prices of unhusked rice, yellow corn, soybeans, and mung beans, increasing farmers' incomes so they could better cope with the policy change.

1. Robert Repetto, "Economic Policy Reform for Natural Resource Conservation," Environment Working Paper (Washington, D.C.: World Bank, 1988).

2. Theodore Panayotou, "Natural Resources and the Environment in the Economies of Asia and the Near East: Growth, Structural Change and Policy Reform" (Cambridge, Mass.: Harvard Institute for International Development, 1989), mimeo.

3. Gordon R. Conway, Ibrahim Manwan, and David S. McCauley, *The Sustainability of Agricultural Intensification in Indonesia: A Report of Two Workshops of the Research Group on Agro-Ecosystems* (Jakarta: Ford Foundation and Agency for Agricultural Research and Development, Ministry of Agriculture, Indonesia, 1984).

4. Edward B. Barber, *Economics, Natural Resource Scarcity, and Development* (London: Earthscan Publications, 1989).

5. Panayotou, "Natural Resources and the Environment in the Economies of Asia and the Near East."

6. Ibid.

7. Food and Agriculture Organization (FAO), *Integrated Pest Management in Rice in Indonesia* (Jakarta: FAO, 1988).

8. "Government to Abolish Subsidy for Utilization of Pesticide," *The Jakarta Post*, December 2, 1988.

others. Macroeconomic policies fail when they lack micro-economic foundations (such as liberalization in the absence of functioning markets) or ignore significant environmental consequences (such as the effects of high interest rates, overvalued exchange rates, or excessive borrowing on natural resource depletion). I will now address these three kinds of policy failure in more detail.

Project-related Policy Failures

Project policies refer to both public and private projects. Public projects are a potent instrument of government intervention for mitigating market failures by providing public goods such as roads, utilities, and parks. If used inappropriately, however, they can become a major source of market distortion. First, since most public projects are financed directly or indirectly from general taxation, they tend to crowd out private investment as well as to redistribute resources. This is justified and beneficial only to the extent that public projects generate higher economic and social returns than private projects. Second, public projects, especially in developing countries, tend to be very large compared with both private projects and the size of the economy. Because of their sheer size and their infrastructural nature, public projects tend to have large effects on both the economy and the environment. Therefore, taking prices as given and ignoring environmental and social effects is a recipe for failure.

Infrastructure projects such as roads and irrigation systems often have environmental effects that extend far beyond the physical displacement of natural environments and any associated spillovers. For example, the environmental impact of road construction through an undisturbed forest is not simply the forest cut to make room for the road, or even the damage to the environment from road traffic and air pollution. The single largest environmental impact comes from the increased encroachment on or colonization of the forest facilitated by the road, as the Trans-Amazon Highway through Accre and Rondonia amply demonstrated. A multimillion-dollar project in the name of national development has resulted in unprecedented rates of encroachment and deforestation and little sustainable economic benefit.

Two other examples come from Thailand. Only fifteen years ago the lower northeast region of Thailand was covered with undisturbed forest. Then the state constructed a major highway. According to Thailand's National Economic and Social Development Board: "Landless farmers . . . from around the area and elsewhere have moved in and cleared the land for cultivation, resulting in the destruction of forest land (and watersheds) of 5.28 million rai (one million ha) between 1973 and 1977. The sporadic immigration to clear new land for cultivation has given birth to 318 villages in the past nine years."[2] Today the area is devastated by salinization and soil erosion that make both forestry and agriculture unsustainable. Had private and communal property rights been issued before the road opened, both agriculture and forestry could be sustainable.

Another example comes from the Nam Pong multipurpose reservoir-irrigation system constructed in 1966 in northeast Thailand. Like the highway, the watershed area of the reservoir attracted large numbers of people, both those who were displaced from the reservoir area and those who came from other areas to the reservoir, which unexpectedly developed a productive fishery with more than seventy edible species. The influx of people into the area led to rapid deforestation of the open-access watershed, increased soil erosion, and sedimentation of the reservoir. The results were harm to the reservoir fishery, reduced power generation, and a diminished capacity for irrigation and flood control (see Case 5 on page 24).

Some blame population growth, a proximate rather than the ultimate cause of deforestation, and prescribe population control. But this would amount to little more than treatment of symptoms, since in the case of both the dam and the highway, the influx of population would have not taken place to the degree it did in the absence of the project. Prescribing population control as a remedy to a problem caused by poor project planning, by failure to establish secure property rights over agricultural and forest lands, and by failure to recognize externalities and internalize the environmental cost of the project is tantamount to arguing that no matter what the market and

CASE 9

Policy Failure: The Logging Ban in Thailand

In November 1988 Thailand was struck by catastrophic flooding and landslides that killed 350, left 70,000 homeless, and caused millions of dollars of damage to farms and fisheries. While seemingly a natural disaster, the floods were in fact the result of both changes in land-use patterns (where cash crops such as rubber have replaced less-erosive ground cover) and rampant logging by villagers and large companies. Indeed, Thailand's forest cover is 20 percent today compared with over 60 percent in the 1950s.[1]

In response to the disaster, the Thai government banned all commercial logging nationwide. The ban, however, has largely failed to reduce deforestation. In fact, deforestation may have *increased* since the ban was imposed. The local press in June 1989 reported more serious deforestation since the ban, as documented by a Forestry Department survey. Aerial surveys recorded a 54 percent increase in deforested land between January and May 1989 compared with the same period in 1988. Also, illegal logging was uncovered in 2,500 forests compared with 1,300 forests a year earlier.[2]

Although the logging ban may appear to address directly the problem of deforestation in Thailand,[3] the underlying incentives for land clearing for agriculture remain firmly in place—which may be the reason the logging continues.[4] These root causes include a fast-growing population, which leads to social pressures such as increased rural poverty and lack of employment opportunities. The agriculture minister admitted that logging violations were committed almost wholly by villagers as a way to supplement income. The Thai government's response to these pressures has been tacit encouragement of the landless peasants' squatting on forest lands. In some cases, the government's support has been more overt. For example, 1.2 million landless families have been resettled on "deteriorated" forest land in the past decade. Authorities, however, have not allowed the landless migrants to secure firm land ownership.

Indeed, half-measures such as the granting of twenty-five-year usufruct rights to squatters on public forest lands encourage further encroachment, without investing farmers with the long-term interests needed to stimulate more effective and sustainable land management. Depriving farmers of access to formal credit or other investment incentives leads to myopic planning or no planning at all. Insecure land tenure dominates more than 50 percent of Thailand, leaving farmers with few options other than to "mine" the land, since more sustainable land management practices will not be rewarded.[5] A logging ban does not address these underlying causes of deforestation. Until issues of land tenure, employment opportunities, and rural poverty are resolved, deforestation and subsequent flooding and landslides will continue to plague Thailand.

---

1. Meri McCoy-Thompson, "Sliding Slopes Break Thai Logjam," *World Watch* (September/October 1989).

2. Apisak Dhanasetthakarn, "More Deforestation since Logging Ban," *The Nation* (June 29, 1989).

3. Deforestation is estimated to be at 3 percent per year; Edith Mirante, "A 'Teak War' Breaks Out in Burma," *Earth Island Journal* (Summer 1989).

4. Steven Erlanger, "Indonesia Takes Steps to Protect Rain Forests," *New York Times* (September 26, 1989).

5. Theodore Panayotou, "Thailand's Management of Natural Resources for Sustainable Development: Market Failures, Policy Distortions and Policy Options," (Cambridge, Mass.: Harvard Institute for International Development, 1988), mimeo.

policy failures involved, without people there would have been no problem! In any case, Thailand over the past twenty years has undergone the most spectacular reduction in population growth of any country, from over 3 percent in the late 1960s to under 1.5 percent today through voluntary incentives, education, and economic growth. It is true that northeast Thailand continues to be relatively densely populated and poor, but this is not because of high population growth but because of skewed economic growth (centered in the central region), barriers to mobility (insecure land ownership, inappropriate education policy), and distorted sector markets that favor capital intensity in industry at the expense of labor employment.

An econometric study of the causes of deforestation in northeast Thailand found that population density (as distinct from population growth), poverty, and infrastructure (dams and roads), as well as economic incentives (wood and crop prices), played a significant role in deforestation.[3]

Public projects are usually justified economically through cost-benefit analysis, which in principle should consider all social benefits and costs, monetary or not, quantifiable or not. Project-level distortions or biases against efficient resource use, environmental quality, and sustainable development can arise for one of the following reasons: (1) projects are selected based on financial appraisal (cash flows) or narrow economic analysis (shadow pricing some inputs and not others); (2) the social benefits and costs are too narrowly defined in space and time (they exclude externalities and long-term effects); (3) the environmental effects are unforeseen at the design stage of the project; (4) the environmental costs are foreseen and appreciated, but it is difficult to measure and evaluate them; (5) an unduly high social discount rate is used; and (6) the irreversibility of project-induced changes in the environment is ignored or not properly handled.

Although difficulties remain, in recent years researchers have developed sophisticated techniques for evaluating environmental externalities and incorporating them into cost-benefit analysis. Regarding the discount rate, two points are important. First, the discount rate does not discriminate against environmental benefits per se but rather against long-term benefits that may be development benefits. Second, the discount rate is a public policy parameter that can help promote a longer-term perspective as long as it is used consistently and with full appreciation of the fact that the lower the social discount rate, compared with the market discount rate, the more private investment will be crowded out by public projects.[4]

The emphasis on projects rather than on investment programs, economic policies, and development strategies is in itself a major policy distortion. Governments focus on choosing among projects rather than on asking whether anything needs to be done in a given resource area. Similarly, they concentrate on designing and implementing new projects rather than on evaluating how well projects have fared in the past. Peter Rogers describes this bias in the case of water resource policies:

In most countries the framework for interrelating national economic policies with water resource policies has been collapsed down to an accounting framework whereby the possible investments in the water sector are analyzed project by project. These projects are added together to make a portfolio of investments offered by the technical agencies to the planning commission as the investment policy. The planning commission then responds by checking to see if the overall resources demanded can be met from the available current, or projected, economic resources. The planning commission then either recommends changes or passes the portfolio on to the executive for approval. Depending upon the country, and the time and resources available to it, the planning commission may, or may not, check for consistency between the water sector and the other sectors of the economy.[5]

Planning paradigms can be quite effective if the planners have sufficient time to go back and forth between economic sectors two or three times during the process. In actual planning situations, however, time is scarce. The result is a one-sided, one-directional analysis: the effects of a project in one sector (or in part of a sector) on the economic policies are assessed, but the reverse is typically not done. Therefore, real assessments of the value of investments in the water sector are never effectively compared with those in other sectors. The enormous investments in irrigation systems throughout the developing world

CASE 10

Turning a Market Failure into a Policy Success:
Improving Security of Land Ownership in Thailand

As a result of massive forest encroachment and land clearing for agriculture since the early 1970s, 37 percent of the agricultural land in Thailand is undocumented and untitled. Another 47 percent is covered by certificates granting temporary use. The lack of secure ownership of land constitutes a serious obstacle to farm investments necessary for diversification, intensification, and increased productivity. Untitled or temporarily held land is not accepted by financial institutions as collateral for credit. As a result, farmers are forced into the informal credit market, where high interest rates make farm investments unprofitable.[1] The risk of eviction, however small, adds an element of uncertainty that further discourages investments in land improvements and soil conservation. Uncertainty, lack of access to institutional credit, and easy access to public forest land combine to bias agricultural development against intensification on existing lands and in favor of expansion into new lands.

There is empirical evidence that insecurity of ownership has been a serious impediment to production growth in Thailand. According to a 1988 study by Gershon Feder and others, "Large numbers of farmers do not have legal ownership of the land which they operate even though they are perceived as *de facto* owners within the farming community."[2] Using extensive surveys and rigorous econometric analysis, the Feder study found that (1) the value of insecurely held land was only one-half to two-thirds the value of securely owned comparable land, and (2) the capital-land ratio in securely owned lands was 60–250 percent higher than that of insecurely titled land. Finally, the authors found that the social benefits from providing land ownership security range from 25 to 80 percent of the market value of the squatters' land and that the private benefits to the farmers were even higher. These are enormous benefits, if one considers that almost 40 percent of the agricultural land in Thailand is untitled. They amount to roughly 10–30 percent growth in Thailand's total agricultural productivity and could contribute to substantial soil and forest conservation. It is believed that 14 percent of the encroached forest in northern Thailand is used to replace land that is seriously eroded and degraded.[3]

With assistance from the World Bank, the government of Thailand is currently carrying out a major land titling program to improve farmers' security of land ownership. Unfortunately, the government gives squatters in reserved forest lands only nontransferable rights to farm ranging from five to twenty-five years, because it fears that granting them full titles might encourage them to sell their land for a song and continue opening new land in reserved forests. It is more likely, however, that the half-measure of use rights will lead to further forest encroachment since the Feder study found that only full, secure, exclusive, transferable, and indefinite titles to land could result in increased investment and higher productivity.

1. Gershon Feder, Tongroj Onchan, Yongyuth Chalamwong, and Chira Hongladarom, *Land Policies and Farm Productivity in Thailand* (Baltimore: Johns Hopkins University Press for the World Bank, 1988).

2. Ibid.

3. P. Attaviroj, "Soil Erosion and Degradation in Northern Thai Upland: An Economic Study," paper presented at the International Conference on the Economics of Dry Land Degradation and Rehabilitation, Canberra, March 10–14, 1986.

in the past forty years were rarely seen in the context of a national development policy, or even an agricultural or water policy. Otherwise, the protection of the watersheds and provisions for system maintenance, water distribution, and drainage would not have been neglected. Similarly, in the context of a national or rural development policy, the construction of roads through forests without prior clarification of land rights would not have taken place.

The bias for or against projects as opposed to policies is not unique to government agencies. Environmental groups have focused on the environmental damage caused by projects such as Nam Choan Dam in Thailand, the Narmada multipurpose dam in India, and the Tucurui Dam in Brazil, rather than on the massive market failures and policy distortions that lead to wholesale destruction of natural resources and degradation of the environment. When projects are seen as part of an overall development policy, many of the externalities now unaccounted for would be internalized and much of the development-environment conflict resolved. Many developing economies are far from their efficient production frontier. It is certainly feasible to produce more development and a better environment at the same time by correcting market failures and eliminating policy distortions. This is the context in which public projects should be planned, designed, and evaluated.

Sectoral Policy Failures

Forest Policies

Forest policy is an excellent example of a resource-specific policy that must be overhauled if the link between scarcity and prices is to be reestablished. If indeed we are facing a growing scarcity of forests, forest product prices should be rising to slow down deforestation and accelerate reforestation. At present, not only are most forest products and services not priced, but even timber, an internationally tradable commodity, is priced below its true scarcity value because of implicit and explicit subsidies and institutional failures (see Tables 3 and 4). Uncollected resource rents, subsidized logging on marginal and fragile forest lands, and volume-based taxes on timber removal

TABLE 3

Government Rent Capture in Tropical Timber Production, 1979–1982 (millions of US$)

Country or region	Potential rent	Actual rent	Official government rent captured	Rent captured as % of actual rent	Rent captured as % of potential rent
Indonesia	4,958	4,409	1,654	37.5	33.0
Sabah region of Malaysia	2,065	2,064	1,703	82.5	82.5
Philippines	1,504	1,001	141	14.0	9.4

SOURCE: Robert Repetto, "Economic Policy Reform for Natural Resource Conservation," Environment Working Paper (Washington, D.C.: World Bank, May 1988).

TABLE 4

Stumpage Fees and Replacement Costs for Selected Developing Countries

Country (currency)	Estimated stumpage fees per cubic meter	Replacement cost per cubic meter	Stumpage fees as % of replacement cost
Ethiopia (Birr)	4	8–19	22–48
Kenya (KSh)			
Deadwood collected by headload	2–5	n.a.	n.a.
Purchases by concessionaires	19	58	33
Malawi (MK)			
Government plantations	3	18	16
Private plantations	3	5	58
Niger (CFAF)	85	13,610	1
Rwanda (Fr)	160	600	27
Senegal (CFAF)	185	9,250	2
Sudan (LS)			
Bushland	n.a.	10–46	n.a.
Low rainfall savannah	n.a.	6–28	n.a.
High rainfall savannah	n.a.	2–9	n.a.
Tanzania (TSh)			
Plantation poles	60–88	66	91–133
Bush poles	20–30	30	67–100
Fuelwood plantation	12	25	48
Fuelwood brush	6	9	67

n.a. = not available.
SOURCE: Robert Repetto, "Economic Policy Reform for Natural Resource Conservation," Environment Working Paper (Washington, D.C.: World Bank, May 1988).

encourage high grading[6] and destructive logging. Forest concessions are typically too short to provide incentives for conservation and replanting. Failure to value nontimber goods and services results in excessive deforestation, conflicts with local communities, loss of economic value, and environmental damage. Promotion of local processing of timber often leads to inefficient plywood mills, excess capacity, waste of valuable tropical timber, and loss of government revenues. Replanting subsidies often end up subsidizing the conversion of a valuable natural forest to inferior monospecies plantations, with the associated loss of the value of both tropical hardwoods and biological diversity.

Results of these policy failures are clear in Honduras. At current rates of deforestation, forestry resources in Honduras will be exhausted within a quarter of a century. More specifically, Honduras is witnessing large-scale destruction of pine and broadleaf forests. As a result of this severe deforestation, an estimated 10,000 hectares of tillable soil is being lost annually. Furthermore, the resulting watershed destruction has imposed heavy social and economic costs in terms of siltation, flooding, shortening of the useful life of reservoirs, and loss of productive capacity. Both insecure land tenure and inefficient forestry resource pricing have been implicated as root causes of Honduran deforestation. Policies of the public forest corporation (COHDEFOR) have encouraged excessive rates of extraction and dampened incentives for long-run investment in the forestry sector. Meanwhile, farmers who are denied access to fertile lands are increasingly turning to marginal areas for farming, leading to highly destructive slash-and-burn techniques.[7]

Concerns over rapid rates of deforestation and slow rates of replanting have given rise to export bans on unprocessed timber by tropical timber producers such as Thailand, the Philippines, and Indonesia. The primary motivation in Thailand has been the conservation of forest resources, and in Indonesia, an increase in value added through domestic processing and, by implication, forest conservation. The log export bans have largely failed to slow deforestation in all three countries. In Thailand and the Philippines, illegal logging and clearing of land for permanent and shifting cultivation have continued unabated. In Indonesia, the inefficient and excessive processing capacity stimulated by the log export ban has led to logging rates above the pre-ban levels.

Following the catastrophic landslides and floods of November 1988 that were attributed to deforestation, the Thai government introduced an indefinite logging ban. This is a well-meant and popular action. Unless it is supplemented with effective enforcement and forest management, however, it is unlikely to succeed in stemming the rate of deforestation. Illegal logging, encroachment, and shifting cultivation are likely to continue and even intensify in the absence of the logging concessions, because population pressures, poverty, and incentives for opening land for agriculture have not changed. Nor has the enforcement capability of the Department of Forestry, the legal owner of these forests, improved. Already, there have been controversial reports in the local press that the rate of deforestation increased following the imposition of the ban in January 1989 (see Case 9 on page 68).

Land Policies

Insecurity of land ownership is the single most severe policy failure in developing countries. It prevents the optimal use of land and leads to the degradation of land, water, and forest resources. Insecurity of land ownership takes many forms: untitled land, the result of forest encroachment and squatting; land under unclear, disputed, or multiple ownership; land under short-term lease or tenancy; land that may be subject to land reform or appropriation; land under usufruct or stewardship certificates that are temporary and nontransferable; and land whose ownership is tied to compulsory state trading, price controls, and forced cooperatives through which the "owner" is forced to buy inputs at higher than market prices and to sell outputs at lower than market prices.

Untitled or insecurely held land is commonly found in the Philippines and Thailand (as a result of shifting cultivation), in Indonesia (as a result of spontaneous migration), in Myanmar (in areas outside the control of the central government), in Nepal (as a result of migration from the hills to the Terrai), and in Africa (in tribal lands). The most common form of insecure tenure in the Philippines and South Asia is tenancy. While owners and tenants with reasonable security do not seem to differ in their willingness to adopt innovations, such as new varieties, fertilizers, and pesticides for annual crops, they may have different attitudes toward long-term investments that enhance land productivity and sustainability over the long run, such as irrigation and drainage structures, land terracing, and tree crops.[8]

A classic example of multiple or unclear ownership is provided by some 500,000 tanks and ponds covering 70,000 hectares in land-scarce Bangladesh that remain largely unused despite an apparent high potential for fish culture.[9] Widespread multiple joint ownership aggravated by joint inheritance by descendants may be a major constraint.[10] Similarly, open-access pastures are clearly an extreme case of multiple ownership, but communally managed lands or pastures are not if the community has sufficient cohesion, social organization, and leadership to make decisions about optimal use. This is why communal and tribal lands in Papua New Guinea (see Case 4 on page 20) and in parts of Africa do not suffer from insecurity of ownership while in other parts of Africa insecurity is pervasive. In fact, there are examples from northern Thailand, India, and Kenya and several other African countries where tribal land in one village is managed almost as if it is owned by a single individual, while in a neighboring village it is exploited as open-access land, with the well-known consequences of the "tragedy of the commons."

In Lesotho, for example, the most striking examples of environmental degradation are the related problems of severe soil erosion and severe overgrazing of mountainous pasture lands. Because of a lack of secure and enforceable grazing rights, farmers rush to exploit pasture lands with little thought for the future. This insecure land tenure leads to overstocking of animals and consequent overexploitation and degradation of pasture land. The problem is exacerbated by wage remittances from Basotho miners, which inject excess liquidity into the local economy. Lack of attractive investment alternatives induces farmers to invest in additional livestock in an effort to increase their share of a shrinking resource.[11]

The lack of secure ownership of land constitutes a serious

obstacle to farm investments necessary for diversification, intensification, and increased productivity. Untitled land is not accepted by financial institutions as collateral for credit, forcing farmers into the high-interest-rate informal credit market, which makes farm investments unprofitable.[12] The risk of eviction, however small, adds an element of uncertainty that further discourages investments in land improvements and soil conservation. These factors, along with easy access to public forest land, combine to bias agricultural development against intensification on existing lands and in favor of expansion into new lands, which leads to the depletion of forest resources. Moreover, insecurity of land tenure and the consequent lack of access to credit biases the cropping system in favor of annual crops that generate a quick return at the expense of long-term productivity, such as corn and cassava. Tree crops, which may be more profitable over the long run and are certainly more protective of the soil and therefore more sustainable, are discouraged because of their long gestation.

The importance of secure ownership for investment, long-term productivity, and conservation cannot be overemphasized. Based on the World Bank's forty years of experience in lending for agricultural development around the world, Warren C. Baum and Stokes M. Tolbert have concluded that:

> How farmers use land is greatly affected by the degree of security of land-tenure—with respect to such matters as duration of user rights, clarity of land rights, ability to sell these rights or to pass them on to succeeding generations, and ability to obtain compensation for investments. A farmer with unclear, insecure, or short-term tenure is more likely to "mine" the land, that is, to seek maximum short-run production gains through crop rotations and other practices that may degrade the biological and physical qualities of the soil.[13]

The large percentage of agricultural land under insecure tenure in Thailand, the Philippines, Indonesia, and parts of South Asia and Africa is partly due to the open-access status of public forest lands. In the absence of enforcement of state ownership, forest land has been effectively made available for agricultural expansion free of charge. As an unpriced resource, forest land for agricultural expansion is in high demand and increasingly short supply as the limits of the land frontier are being approached. Yet in the absence of secure and transferable titles, an efficient land market for encroached land has failed to develop. Consequently, increasing land scarcity has not led to higher prices and increased land conservation. Thus, a dual market, or rather policy, failure exists. First, an excessive area of forest land is being cleared even when its best use is in forestry rather than in agriculture. Second, cleared land is not used efficiently because of insecure ownership. Moreover, the availability of free land discourages investment even in securely owned lands, because it biases relative prices in favor of extensification and against intensification.

Insecurity of land tenure and lack of access to credit have both on-farm and off-farm environmental consequences that result in further reduction of productivity. The on-farm environmental effects are soil erosion, nutrient leaching, and waterlogging resulting from inadequate incentives (and funds) to invest in drainage and soil conservation practices. The off-farm effects are further encroachment of marginal lands and watersheds because of inability to maintain yields on existing agricultural lands. The results are not only loss of valuable forest resources but also soil erosion and sedimentation of downstream irrigation systems.

Given the consequences of insecurity of land ownership for land productivity, for the owner's income and wealth, and for the quality of the environment, governments have a critical role to play in improving security of ownership. Empirical evidence suggests that the benefits of providing secure titles far exceed the costs.[14] Unfortunately, well-intentioned governments have been exacerbating uncertainty and insecurity by talking about land reform rather than effectively carrying it out, while ignoring other politically more acceptable and economically more efficient means of improving land distribution (such as land taxation).

Graduated, progressive land taxation has been effectively used in Japan to effect land reform without creating the kind of uncertainty that paralyzes long-term investments in the Philippines today.[15] Moreover, since much of the wealth in developing countries is held in the form of land, and land values benefit from rural infrastructure such as roads and irrigation, it is possible and appropriate to use land taxation as the principal source of financing for the operation and maintenance of rural infrastructure. At present, land taxes in many developing countries are nominal and little or no tax revenue is derived from land, partly because of the lack or inadequacy of land cadastre, lack of enforcement, and very low tax rates.

Well-meant government policies that limit property rights to fixed-term use rights and prohibit their transferability or tie the land granted through land reform to state trading, price controls, or forced cooperatives create unnecessary uncertainty and diminish the value of these rights. Such land is not likely to be put to its best use. Concerns about the purchase and accumulation of land by speculators can be dealt with through a land sales tax and a progressive property tax.

Water Policies

A third example of a resource-specific policy that needs to be reformed to reestablish the broken link between scarcity and prices is water policy. Virtually all countries, regardless of the degree of scarcity of water, subsidize water for irrigation and other uses. In many cases they supply it free of charge. Thailand, for instance, experiences droughts and floods seasonally in some areas and continually in others. Northeast Thailand suffers from perennial water shortages. The central region is inundated in the rainy season and imports water from the northern region in the dry season. Only 30 percent of the irrigable area covered by the Greater Chao Phraya Project has adequate irrigation in the dry season. Yet this profound and growing water scarcity does not register. According to Thailand's *Natural Resources Profile*, "many farmers continue to think of water as a free, virtually unlimited resource whereas the facts increasingly suggest otherwise."[16] Irrigation water is provided free of charge without any attempt to recover cost or to charge a price reflecting the scarcity value or opportunity cost of water. The result is overirrigation with consequent salinization and waterlogging in some areas and inadequate water in others. This gross waste of water limits the efficiency of irrigation systems to about 15 percent of a potential of 60 to 70 percent,[17] while the failure to achieve any degree of cost recovery deprives the system of operation and maintenance funds.

Similar problems of growing water scarcity are found in Indonesia, which ranks second in Asia and the Near East in terms of freshwater endowment. Densely populated Java faces increasing water shortages that are being addressed through supply rather than demand management. But the area facing the most critical water scarcity is the Near East. According to Elias Saleh, a hydrologist with Jordan University, "In the mid 1990s farmers in the high plains and in the swelter of the Jordan Valley will face a crisis because the growing population will lay claim to water for drinking, and irrigation will be curtailed. . . . Water is the future of the whole area. . . . It is very critical."[18] Virtually all Near East countries, but particularly Egypt, Yemen, Jordan, and Tunisia, face severe water shortages, yet water continues to be subsidized throughout the region, and water efficiency is unacceptably low. In Egypt, where 30 percent of the irrigated lands suffer from salinization and waterlogging due to overirrigation, "efficiency ratings will have to increase by 60 percent over the next 11 years to meet the needs of the population, projected to reach 70 million in the year 2000."[19] According to the same source, "Jordan is expecting a water crisis within a decade and a dearth of new water resources by the year 2005."

Urbanization and Industrialization

Industrial development and urbanization are highly correlated. Industries in many developing countries, and some developed ones, are often located in or near urban centers because of the skewed distribution of public infrastructure (such as roads, electricity, telephones, and government offices). About half of the industrial value added of countries as diverse as Brazil, Thailand, and Egypt comes from industries located in their largest urban centers (see Case 11 on page 84). Correspondingly, industrial pollution is concentrated in and around urban centers like São Paulo, Bangkok, and Cairo. Thus, it is often difficult to determine what part of observed environmental degradation is caused by industrialization and what part by urbanization.

The plight of Santo Domingo illustrates the problems many cities face. Several sections of Santo Domingo suffer from severe air pollution due to emissions from a scrap iron factory, a cement factory, and electric power plants. Unenforceable zoning regulations and successful lobbying by industrial concerns to avoid relocation and installation of emission-controlling devices have made pollution control efforts ineffective. Moreover, Santo Domingo's slums are teeming and the quality of life there is rapidly deteriorating. Neither the private nor the public sector has been able to provide adequate housing, food, electrical power, water, education, or employment opportunities. The government in fact encourages migration since public works are concentrated in urban areas, while rural infrastructure is sorely lacking.[20]

Increased urbanization and industrialization in the 1990s will exacerbate already serious problems of crowding and water and air pollution in cities such as Manila, Bangkok, Jakarta, Delhi, Calcutta, Cairo, Casablanca, Mexico City, and São Paulo (see Table 5). Consequently, more attention and resources must be devoted to addressing urban environmental problems than in the past.

To employ the growing labor force, governments are likely to place more emphasis on industrial development in the 1990s, thus increasing the production and disposal of hazardous toxic chemicals and wastes. This is already a major problem in India, Thailand, the Philippines, Egypt, Mexico, and Brazil. Similarly, the intensification of agriculture to accommodate more people on the same amount of land will inevitably lead to increased use of toxic agricultural chemicals, which presents a new set of problems for policy makers. Indonesia has already experienced a crisis related to the use of agricultural pesticides. The disastrous leakage of industrial hazardous chemicals from the plant in Bhopal, India, is another example of the risks developing countries face.

Industrialization is certain to have environmental implications, not only for urban centers but also for rural areas. The impact of industrialization on the rural environment will depend on labor intensity, location, and type of industry.

CASE 11

The Costs of Air Pollution in São Paulo, Brazil

Known as the "Valley of Death" because of the effect of its air pollution on residents, the Greater São Paulo Area (GSPA) dramatically illustrates the possible outcome when the social costs of industrialization and vehicle use are ignored. With an area of 8,000 square kilometers, the GSPA is one of the largest metropolitan areas in the world. It produces more than 40 percent of Brazil's industrial value added. In 1981, its population of 11 million was growing at a rate of 5–6 percent.[1]

This dense population and concentration of heavy industry have given rise to levels of air pollution often well above maximum "acceptable" standards. Emissions for the entire GSPA are estimated at seven thousand tons per day, over half of which is carbon monoxide. Nearly three-quarters of the air pollution, including almost all of the carbon monoxide, is produced by cars, with most of the rest created by industry. In 1978, daily air-quality standards for carbon monoxide alone were exceeded 299 times, at times by a factor of nearly three. With air pollution and population densities varying widely from municipality to municipality, air pollution levels exceed standards more frequently and by greater amounts in the most densely populated areas. Not surprisingly, the residents in these areas also suffer more from pollution-related health problems.[2]

Although the health effects in São Paulo are painfully visible, quantifying the economic costs of air pollution is difficult. In addition to the impact on humans, damage to property, equipment, farm animals, and crops must be included. A number of studies have successfully correlated health damages from pollution with levels of industrial concentration and population density in the different GSPA municipalities. In one such study, Fernicola and Azevedo have linked average levels of lead in the blood of residents to the level of air pollution in different municipalities. Examining a two-week period in 1973, Rene Mendes found a close correlation between sulfur dioxide concentrations and deaths due to respiratory diseases in the GSPA. Upon studying the relationship between pollution and mortality in São Paulo, a World Bank report concluded that "an annual increase of 1 ton of particulates per km^2 in the GSPA from 1977 levels is associated with an increase in the mortality rate of 12 per million."[3]

Attempts to limit air pollution are in the fledgling stages at the federal, state, and municipal levels. Using air-quality standards delineated by the federal government to calculate necessary abatements, the states have set emission standards for different sources of air pollution. Both the federal and state governments are also using licensing and zoning to try to control existing and potential new sources of pollution. At the municipal level, the GSPA has employed land-use policy to limit the location of new industries and the levels of allowable pollution in different areas.

In the GSPA, reducing air pollution to the federal standards will require abatements of 80 to 90 percent. The World Bank and the state's environmental agency, CETESB, estimate the annual cost of a 55 percent reduction at US$6 million, or US$1.10 to US$1.20 per resident affected by the pollution.[4] Given the impact of pollution on health, the CETESB has judged the benefits to more than justify this level of expenditure. The cost of abatement, however, clearly depends on the efficiency of the controls levied. Pollution standards or taxes are more efficient than mandatory control equipment, fuel restrictions, or output restrictions, because the former give polluters the flexibility to choose the most cost-effective method of abatement for their firm. In the case of taxes, firms also determine the value of their right to pollute and whether abatement is an efficient choice.[5]

1. Vinod Thomas, "Pollution Control in São Paulo, Brazil: Costs, Benefits, and Effects on Industrial Location," World Bank Staff Working Paper No. 501 (Washington, D.C.: World Bank, 1981).

2. Ibid.

3. These studies are described in Thomas, "Pollution Control in São Paulo, Brazil."

4. Hans P. Binswanger, "Brazilian Policies That Encourage Deforestation in the Amazon" (Washington, D.C.: World Bank, 1989).

5. Thomas, "Pollution Control in São Paulo, Brazil."

TABLE 5

Urbanization in Developing Countries, 1950–2000

Region	Population living in urban areas (% of total population)		
	1950	1985	2000
World	29.2	41.0	46.6
Africa	15.7	29.7	39.0
Latin America	41.0	69.0	76.8
Temperate South America	64.8	84.3	88.6
Tropical South America	35.9	70.4	79.4
Asia	16.4	28.1	35.0
China	11.0	20.6	25.1
India	17.3	25.5	34.2

City	Population of selected cities (millions of people)		
	1950	Most recent data	2000[a]
Mexico City	3.05	16.0 (1982)	26.3
São Paulo	2.7	12.6 (1980)	24.0
Bombay	3.0	8.2 (1981)	16.0
Jakarta	1.45	6.2 (1977)	12.8
Cairo	2.5	8.5 (1979)	13.2
Delhi	1.4	5.8 (1981)	13.3
Manila	1.78	5.5 (1980)	11.1
Lagos	0.27	4.0 (1980)	8.3
Bogotá	0.61	3.9 (1985)	9.6
Nairobi	0.14	0.8 (1979)	5.3
Dar Es Salaam	0.15	0.9 (1981)	4.6
Greater Khartoum	0.18	1.1 (1978)	4.1
Amman	0.03	0.8 (1978)	1.5

a. United Nations projection.
Source: World Commission on Environment and Development, *Our Common Future* (Oxford: Oxford University Press, 1987).

Combined with the appropriate location and educational policy, labor-intensive industry is likely to attract labor out of the marginal and fragile areas and thus reduce the pressure on natural resources. Capital-intensive industry has a limited effect on employment and rather extensive effects on the rural environment through its demand for materials and energy and the generation of pollutants such as acid rain and water effluents.

Urban environmental quality is clearly an area of massive market failures. The urban environment is an unpriced common property resource. Environmental pollution is a public externality whose internalization involves prohibitively high transaction costs because of the millions of polluters and affected parties involved. Pollution abatement and its product, environmental quality, are public goods that cannot be provided by a free market. Because no one can be excluded from receiving the benefits of pollution abatement, no one will finance it.

Although the increasing regulation of industrial pollution shows a growing recognition of environmental problems in urban centers around the world, the environment is still treated by both households and industries as an open-access space for free disposal of wastes. In many countries, large industries are required to submit environmental impact studies before their establishment and meet certain emission standards during their operation, but effective enforcement is lacking. Moreover, the far more numerous small industries and millions of households continue to enjoy free disposal of waste into the environment. Urban centers in developing countries lack sewage treatment facilities. Public and private automobiles emit air and noise pollution without restriction. Farmers release water contaminated with toxic fertilizers and pesticides into the main water sources. This free disposal of wastes is tantamount to a lack of property rights over the environment or use of the scarce assimilative capacity of the environment free of charge. Unpriced or open-access resources are overused, underconserved, and mismanaged.

In Yemen, for example, waste management problems abound. Some areas, both urban and rural, are literally buried in plastic bottles. A tree covered with plastic bags is a frequent sight and is sometimes jokingly referred to as Yemen's "national tree." Toxic waste from industrial plants has been tied to water contamination, and improper storage and use of toxic pesticides and herbicides are continuing threats.[21]

As countries become increasingly industrialized and urbanized, the environment is used beyond its assimilative capacity to dispose of the by-products of economic activity, and, as a consequence, environmental quality deteriorates. Even agriculture, usually thought of as more benign to the environment than industry, is becoming a major source of pollution as it becomes more intensified through the use of mechanical and chemical inputs such as toxic fertilizers, pesticides, and fossil fuels. At the same time, as the supply of clean environment declines, the demand for environmental quality rises as a result of income growth. Thus, while the significance of forests, land, and water as inputs into the production process may decline somewhat with industrialization, urbanization, and agricultural intensification, their significance as assimilators of industrial, urban, and agricultural waste and as sources of environmental amenities is certain to rise.

Further industrialization and agricultural intensification, however, will not necessarily cause further environmental degradation. The level of pollution depends on the types of new or expanded industries, their spatial distribution, their input mix and technology, and the incentive structure and environmental regulations introduced by the government.

Many governments choose a direct regulatory approach, under which the government sets effluent or emission standards—maximum permissible levels of discharge of each pollutant from each source—and relies on administrative agencies and the judicial system to enforce them. An alternative or supplementary standard is the ambient standard, which sets the minimum acceptable level of environmental quality for a receiving water source or airshed. In the United States, both standards are used to control water pollution, in combination with heavy subsidies for construction of waste treatment facilities.

Incentives such as tax write-offs, accelerated depreciation, low-interest loans, or outright subsidies for the adoption of "clean" production technologies or the construction of waste treatment facilities are inefficient and ineffective. They do not make waste reduction or waste treatment any more profitable; they simply subsidize the producers and consumers of the products of these industries. In any case, waste treatment is not always the most efficient means of reducing wastes. Often, changing production processes, the type and quality of raw materials, or the rate of output is more efficient. In some instances rearrangement of the production process can result in both reduction of waste and recovery of valuable by-products, such as fertilizer from palm oil extraction and syrup from fruit canning. Tax breaks, credits, depreciation allowances, and subsidies are therefore a disincentive to industries that might otherwise develop more efficient methods for reducing emissions as well as a drain on the government budget.

Direct regulation and subsidization suffer from many other weaknesses. They rely on centralized setting and enforcement of standards, which is both costly and ineffective. They promote inefficiency, since they require similar reduction of pollution from all sources regardless of costs. They emphasize subsidized end-of-the-pipe, capital-intensive solutions, such as waste treatment plants. They result in large bureaucracies and costly subsidies. They require that the environmental agency master the technologies of both production and pollution control for hundreds of different types of industries and all their technological alternatives, a monumental task that detracts from the agency's principal monitoring functions. In addition, the environmental agency must engage in endless negotiations with the polluters over the type of equipment to be installed, resulting in long delays and compromise of the agency's standards. Compliance is generally limited because the certainty-equivalent amount of the fine (amount of the fine times the probability of detection times the probability of conviction) for noncompliance is only a fraction of the cost of compliance in terms of expensive abatement equipment and loss of competitive position. The moral hazards of "regulatory capture" (in which the regulators are coopted by the regulated) and bribing of enforcement officials are higher than in any other pollution control system because of the protracted negotiations and ambiguity of compliance to the set standards. Finally, direct regulation provides ample opportunity for rent-seeking behavior.

Urban congestion and pollution increasingly dominate the life of large urban centers. Bangkok's commuters spent an average of 2.5 hours daily in crowded buses and on congested roads. Schoolchildren in Mexico City start school late to avoid the morning smog.[22] Policy responses to congestion problems range from supply management (such as building more roads and introducing one-way traffic) to rationing the use of scarce roads by doing nothing. Supply management works only temporarily: to the extent that congestion is alleviated by new roads, the benefits from driving increase, inducing car owners to drive more and nonowners to purchase cars. As long as open access to city roads prevails, any rents from using them will be driven to zero. This is the basis of rationing by doing nothing: congestion is allowed to become severe enough to discourage any further increase in driving. Such rationing is, however, a very inefficient solution. The costs include loss of productive time, increased use of fossil fuels, increased air pollution (with all the associated health problems, medical bills, and cleaning costs), and increased noise pollution, not to mention frustration and psychic costs. Ultimately those who are left using the roads are those who value their time least (in other words, those who have a low opportunity cost).

My rough calculation of the lost time and increased use of gasoline for Bangkok produced an estimated loss of about US$1.5 billion a year during the late 1980s and early 1990s. Medical bills and days of work lost due to pollution-related ailments, cleaning costs, damage to infrastructure and buildings from increased pollution, and the costs of installing noise insulation and air conditioning in cars and houses may well double this figure. If the total annual cost of congestion is conservatively estimated at US$2.0 billion and this figure is capitalized at a 10 percent interest rate, the present value of the cost of congestion and added pollution in Bangkok is US$20 billion. Just a fraction of this amount would suffice to provide Bangkok with a clean, efficient, and rapid mass transport system. Charges for the use of city center roads and surcharges on gasoline could be set high enough to hold traffic to levels that would permit it to move freely, and the proceeds could be used to improve public transportation.

Such a system has succeeded elsewhere. Singapore has introduced a road pricing system whereby drivers purchase a permit to enter the city center during rush hours. Buses and car pools are exempted from this requirement, making the system not only efficient but also equitable (see Case 12 on page 92).

Industrial and Trade Policies

Industrial and trade policies may seem only remotely related to natural resource use and management, but they are in fact critical. These policies affect the terms of trade between agriculture and industry and therefore the relative profitability of agriculture and other resource sectors. They are a factor in the use of natural resources as an input in industry. They influence the level of industrial employment and hence the residual rural labor that exerts pressure on natural resources. And they play a role in determining the level of industrial pollution.

Agriculture's terms of trade in most developing countries have deteriorated over the years because these countries have protected industry through import tariffs and investment incentives and taxed agriculture. Adverse terms of trade for agriculture might appear to be conducive to natural resource conservation, since the less profitable agriculture is, the less intensively and extensively land and water resources are used and the less agricultural chemicals are applied. This assumption, however, may not be accurate in labor-abundant economies, dependent on agriculture to employ the majority of the labor force. Reducing the pressure on the agricultural resource base would require moving laborers from agriculture into other sectors. Unfortunately, the increased relative profitability of industry often fails to attract much labor out of agriculture and other resource sectors because of the capital intensity and the urban bias of the promoted industries.

Subsistence farmers and landless unskilled laborers, faced with sliding real incomes due to land shortages (diminishing average holdings) and labor surpluses (low real wages), are in a constant search for supplementary or alternative sources of income. Open-access natural resources such as forests and forest land, inland and coastal fishing grounds, mineral-bearing lands and offshore areas, and the natural environment are the most conveniently accessible sources of supplementary or alternative employment and income. Unemployed household members can earn income by gathering fuelwood and other forest products, fishing, and collecting minerals. Logging illegally, poaching logs, and working for illegal loggers often yield substantially higher income than legal employment, if such can be found. Clearing additional forest land can help maintain and even increase the size of land holdings. Thus, the availability of open-access resources helps halt the drop in incomes resulting from rapid population growth and slow rural development. When open-access resources in the vicinity of a rural community run out, its members migrate to other areas where

CASE 12

Policy Success: Fighting Urban Congestion in Singapore

Like many cities, Singapore has suffered from the environmental effects of an increasing number of cars: congestion resulting in longer travel times for cars and public transport alike, air pollution, wear and tear on roads, and a lower quality of life for those living and working in heavily congested areas. Because car drivers do not naturally bear the substantial costs they impose on society, charging for urban road use is theoretically appealing. The success of Singapore's Area Licensing scheme demonstrates its practical appeal as well.

In 1975 cars represented half of Singapore's 280,000 registered vehicles and were owned at a rate of one per sixteen people. In an attempt to reduce central city traffic by 25–30 percent during peak hours, the city implemented a scheme that charged drivers for using roads in the center of the city during these hours. Specifically, the city aimed to reduce car use within certain areas during particular times, leave economic activity unaffected, enact a scheme that was easy to implement and enforce, and provide those no longer driving into the inner city with attractive travel alternatives. The area pricing scheme required vehicles traveling through the center city at peak hours to purchase a daily or monthly license, raised daytime parking fees within this area, and instituted a park-and-ride service to facilitate easy noncar commuting. Cars with more than four passengers, buses, and motorcycles were exempted from the licensing requirements.[1]

The scheme achieved a traffic reduction of 73 percent in the zone during peak hours. In addition, business seemed largely unaffected. Although the park-and-ride option was not heavily used, the city found the overall scheme easy to enforce and implement. Carpools increased from 10 percent to 40 percent of all traffic, while 13 percent of car-owning commuters into the zone switched to public transit and about the same number changed their commuting time to pre-peak hours. For those who did not change their habits to avoid the zone during peak hours, the average monthly commuting cost rose from US$64 to US$95. More significant, all but one-tenth of "through-zone" commuters changed their route or departure time to avoid licensing fees. Travel speeds increased by 10 percent on incoming roads and by 20 percent on zone roads. Speeds on substitute ring roads increased by 20 percent. The only group experiencing an increase in travel time were converts to public transit, whose average travel time went up by only nine minutes from a previously twenty-nine-minute trip.

The scheme also had environmental benefits. Although other pollutants were difficult to measure, the level of carbon monoxide declined significantly during the hours the scheme was in effect. Central city residents and shoppers reported greater ease and safety in getting around, less fumes, and generally happier living and shopping conditions. Overall, all affected groups concurred that the impact on Singapore was positive. Only motorists perceived themselves as worse off, although not badly so. Their perceptions were accurate since they were, in fact, shouldering more of the social costs of their car use. With an initial return on investment of 77 percent, which, with an increase in license fees, rose to 95 percent, the scheme achieved its goals without undue budgetary costs. Less quantifiable but more significant may be the long-run benefits, the avoidance of future road construction or congestion.

---

1. Much of the material for this case comes from Peter L. Watson and Edward P. Holland, "Relieving Traffic Congestion: The Singapore Area License Scheme," World Bank Staff Working Paper No. 281 (Washington, D.C.: World Bank, 1978).

open-access resources are found. Among the main destinations of these migrants are the major urban centers, where this influx of people results in squatting on public property, creation of slums, crowding, hawking, and general environmental degradation.

The reduced profitability of agriculture as a result of industrial protection also decreases incentives to invest in farmland development and soil conservation, both because of lower returns to such investments and because of limited savings. Moreover, the promotion of industry at the expense of agriculture does not necessarily reduce the use of natural resources. Many industries are indirectly resource based, such as agroprocessing, furniture production, and mineral processing. Industrialization certainly increases energy use both in absolute terms and relative to other inputs, as well as increasing the output of industrial waste. The type of urban-based, capital-intensive industry generally promoted by industrial and trade policies is more resource-intensive (creating more air, water, and noise pollution) at the margin than the low-input agriculture that is being displaced. (Forest land clearing, however, tends to be exacerbated rather than discouraged by industrial policies that limit industrial employment.)

To date, environmental considerations have played little role in the formulation and implementation of industrial and trade policies, partly because the connection has not been obvious and partly because decision makers make policy changes in response to crises or immediate political pressures that do not afford consideration of long-term consequences. In the context of sustainable development, however, ignoring the effects of sectoral and trade policies on resource use and management is self-defeating. For example, protection and credit subsidies for urban-based capital-intensive industries, combined with agricultural taxation to squeeze increasing surpluses out of agriculture and speed up industrialization, may backfire. Because the industry in its early stages depends heavily on agriculture for food, raw materials, foreign exchange, and markets for its products, policies that promote industrialization too heavily at the expense of agriculture undermine the country's industrial base. Equally important, such policies promote inequality, underemployment, and scarcity of rural credit, thereby discouraging investments in land conservation and encouraging encroachment on forest lands. Moreover, the consequent social tensions do not constitute a sound basis for sustainable development.

The most important industrial policy reform necessary is the restoration of the comparative advantage of labor-intensive industry in relation to the highly protected and promoted urban-based capital-intensive manufacturing. The first-best solution would be a sweeping reform of biased industrial and trade policies. For political reasons such reform may not always be feasible. Given the dimensions and the urgency of the employment, poverty, and resource mismanagement problems and the untapped potential of rural industry, a pragmatic second-best policy would be development assistance to rural, labor-intensive industries to create off-farm employment opportunities as an alternative to encroachment and destructive resource exploitation.

To be successful, the promotion of rural industries should build upon the basic features of rural areas: availability of raw materials, seasonality of labor supply, and dispersion of markets. The emphasis should be on restoring a competitive environment between the rural and urban areas by improving infrastructure, making credit available at competitive rates, providing technical assistance and market information, and assisting in skill development.

Three other industrial policies that should be reconsidered in the light of their environmental costs are: (1) depreciation allowances, tax rebates, and tariff exemptions on equipment and materials that might be a major source of pollution, (2) energy subsidies that may favor more-polluting sources of energy over less-polluting ones, and (3) the criteria for approving direct foreign investment (prior screening based on the record of particular firms or industries elsewhere may be more effective than after-the-fact environmental impact assessments).

Macroeconomic Policy Failures

Monetary, fiscal, and exchange rate policies seem even further removed from natural resource management than industrial and trade policies. Yet they may have more powerful effects on how resources are allocated and used than microeconomic or sectoral policies. For example, other things remaining constant, the higher the cost of inputs of capital and labor used in resource extraction or in polluting industries, relative to the price of outputs, the lower the rate of resource depletion and the amount of pollution. If capital-intensive technologies produce more pollution than labor-intensive technologies, the lower the price of capital relative to labor, the more pollution will result. By affecting the prices of capital and labor, macroeconomic policies can help either alleviate or exacerbate environmental degradation.

The rate of interest is an important macroeconomic parameter with microeconomic implications for resource allocation, because it links the present to the future. The higher the interest rate (or discount rate) the higher the cost of waiting; therefore, the faster the rate of resource depletion and the lower the investment in resource conservation. This effect may be mitigated somewhat by the fact that a higher interest rate means a higher cost of capital, which tends to reduce capital-intensive resource depletion and environmental degradation. Promoted industries benefit from interest rate ceilings and implicit interest rate subsidies, while the agricultural sector and the rural economy in general are adversely affected. Credit policy in most developing countries has relied mainly on mandates, quotas, interest rate ceilings, and constrained use of loan proceeds. Yet there is growing evidence that farmers would prefer more flexible terms and increased credit availability even if they had to pay higher interest rates. The liberalization of the capital market is critical to land improvements, reforestation investments, resource conservation, agricultural intensification, and the growth of rural industry.

Because most of the resource-based commodities produced in developing countries are internationally tradable (for example, copper, oil, jute, cotton, tin, fish, rice, beef, rubber, and timber) or are substitutes for tradable commodities (for example, natural gas, lignite, and hydropower), an overvalued exchange rate would reduce their depletion by reducing their price relative to nontradable goods (such as transport, services, and construction). An overvalued exchange rate and export taxes have similar effects in that they discourage exports and encourage imports of resource-based commodities, thereby reducing the pressure on the domestic resource base.

Minimum wage laws, which also encourage capital intensity, reduce labor employment and depress real nonmanufacturing wage rates. Under conditions of labor abundance, these laws lead to increased use of low-cost labor in depleting natural resources and encroachment on resource sectors by unemployed or underemployed labor.

Therefore, even if the problems of open access and externalities are satisfactorily resolved, resource depletion and environmental degradation may continue unless the macroeconomic policies responsible for price distortions in the economy are reformed. The unintended but pronounced effects of fiscal, monetary, and trade policies on natural resources and the environment must enter the assessment and formulation of these policies. The effects of minimum wage rates, subsidized credit, interest rate ceilings, and exchange rate adjustments (along with those of export taxes, investment incentives, and import tariffs) on the rate of resource depletion in a resource-based economy cannot be ignored without endangering the long-term viability of the economy.

It would be unrealistic, however, to expect macroeconomic policies to be tailored to meet environmental objectives given the many other overriding considerations, such as growth stabilization and macroeconomic management, that determine these policies. What can be expected, at best, is that environmental implications are somehow taken into account when these policies are formulated and implemented. Consideration of the resource and environmental implications of macroeconomic policies could have one of several consequences. Environmental costs may tip the scale against marginal policies by raising their social costs above their social benefits; the reverse may happen with policies that have positive environmental effects. Macroeconomic policy interventions might be scaled up or down on account of their environmental implications. Finally, provisions might be made for cushioning the negative environmental effects of policies that cannot be scaled down sufficiently to reduce their environmental cost to acceptable levels.

On the other hand, macroeconomic mismanagement is as detrimental to natural resource management and environmental quality as it is to the other sectors of the economy. Mounting foreign debt, widening trade deficits, hyperinflation, rising interest rates, low savings, negative growth of investments, and growing budget deficits ultimately encourage environmental degradation by causing economic stagnation, increasing poverty, reversing structural adjustments, and shortening the planning horizon (increasing the discount rate). Environmental degradation arising from macroeconomic mismanagement is more common in Africa and Latin America than in Asia.

Structural Adjustment Programs

To help governments restructure their economies to better deal with the emerging problems, the World Bank, the International Monetary Fund (IMF), and other international development agencies have financed structural adjustment loans (SALs) and sectoral adjustment loans (SECALs). For several reasons it is important to consider the effects of these structural and sectoral adjustment loans, and the programs to which they are tied, on resource management and sustainable development. First, these adjustment programs more or less define the macroeconomic and sectoral policies to be followed for much of the 1990s, and, as we have seen, macroeconomic and sectoral policies affect resource allocation and use. Second, since these programs aim to restructure the economies of the region, their effects will extend far beyond the expiration of the programs and loans. Third, for the first time, several countries (both donor and recipient countries) and development assistance agencies have raised environmental concerns in the context of macroeconomic and development policies, and some provisions relating to natural resources and the environment have been included in the loan agreements. Regardless of the adequacy or effectiveness of these provisions, the mere recognition of the implications of macroeconomic, trade, and development policies for the resource base and the environment is a significant step in the right direction. Yet questions have been raised about the overall impact of structural adjustment policies on the environment. I cannot address this topic fully in this study.[23] Because of its importance, however, I will consider for illustration the possible effects of trade, industrial, and agricultural reforms on the environment.

Overall, trade and industrial policy reforms amount to promotion of exports, liberalization of imports, and encouragement of foreign investment. Countries do this by reducing absolute and differential protection, lowering the production and transaction costs of exports and imports, and promoting competition through institutional reform.

The environmental effects of industrial and trade policy reforms taken by themselves are rather ambiguous. On the one hand, to the extent that these policies generate economic growth, create employment, and alleviate poverty, they can help improve the environmental conditions in the country. On the other hand, to the extent that they lead to intensified exploitation and export of natural resources at prices that do not reflect the true resource cost to the country, they lead to deterioration of environmental conditions (timber exports from Indonesia and cassava exports from Thailand are cases in point). Similarly, the environmental effect of accelerated industrialization and foreign investment depends on the type of new industries, their capital and energy intensity, their location, and the enforcement of environmental regulations in the country. In the absence of such regulations and effective enforcement, promotion of low-cost manufactures and encouragement of foreign investment leads to increased industrial pollution. Examples abound, but the cases of Bangkok, Manila, and Cairo will suffice.

Countries can use tariff reform as an opportunity to favor import or manufacture of environmentally benign technologies and machinery and discriminate against highly polluting technologies. To ensure that industrial and trade policy reforms result in relative if not absolute environmental improvement, they can use the import tariff structure to include environmental costs in the pricing of technologies and products. Similarly, environmental conditions should be specified as part of any foreign investment project at the time of application and monitored as part of regular performance evaluation. Such environmental conditions include industrial location, waste disposal, pollution control, accident prevention, and site rehabilitation. Environmental regulations may also be supplemented by emission standards, effluent taxes, or pollution permits. There is a limit, however, to how restrictive a developing country can be and still attract the desired level of foreign investment, since, other things being equal, foreign investment is likely to gravitate to where environmental controls are less restrictive.

Acceptance of increased levels of pollution and other environmental costs in exchange for economic growth, employment, foreign exchange, and government revenues is a legitimate trade-off as long as all environmental costs are internalized. Where environmental costs cannot be adequately internalized into the economic costs and benefits of, for example, foreign investment, there should be explicit determination of the relevant trade-offs. I know of no structural adjustment program that attempts to either internalize environmental costs or determine these important trade-offs.

Agricultural policy reforms related to structural adjustment involve increased producer prices and reduced taxes on agricultural exports to make agricultural production more attractive; changes in relative prices through lower price supports for certain crops (such as sugarcane in Morocco) or reduced taxes for others (such as rice and rubber in Thailand); and reduced agricultural input subsidies to reduce the drain on the budget, save foreign exchange (where inputs are imported), and improve the efficiency of resource use. The environmental effect of such reforms depends on the crops and inputs that are promoted or discouraged and on the institutional context in which the policies are implemented. If land is securely owned and forests are effectively protected and managed, higher prices for agricultural crops in general would lead to more investment in land improvement, soil conservation, and agricultural intensification. Otherwise, the very same policies may lead to increased forest land clearing, cultivation of marginal lands, and agricultural extensification.

Likewise, changes in relative crop prices could benefit or damage the environment depending on the affected crops and the environmental conditions in which they are grown. For example, the reduction of the price support for sugarcane in Morocco has a positive environmental impact because sugarcane is a soil-damaging and water-intensive crop in a water-scarce country. The reduced price support for sugarcane stipulated by Morocco's SAL results not only in less drain on the budget, but also in less pressure on soil and water resources. The market is therefore freer to respond to market signals and shift resources (land and water) to more profitable crops, making better use of limited natural resources with less damage to the environment.

Reduction of export taxes on certain crops such as tree crops helps diversify the economy away from soil-eroding crops such as maize, wheat, or cassava and toward high-value perennial export crops with positive environmental side effects. The irony in the case of Thailand is that high rubber prices and free forest land have encouraged overexpansion of rubber onto steep and fragile slopes, contributing to the catastrophic landslides and floods of 1988 that claimed 350 lives and caused nearly half a billion U.S. dollars in short- and long-term damage. This case clearly demonstrates that economic incentives that have positive environmental effects under certain conditions may be environmentally destructive under a different set of circumstances. Increased incentives for perennial crops such as coffee, cocoa, and rubber relative to annual field crops such as cotton and groundnuts or row crops such as maize and sorghum can help protect the soil on gentle slopes but are not a substitute for natural forest cover on steep or fragile slopes. Countries such as Nepal, Thailand, and Morocco have introduced environmental management programs as part of, or parallel to, their structural adjustment programs.

Reducing agricultural input subsidies, also an integral part of structural adjustment policies, generally has a positive impact on the environment. The Philippines, Nepal, Pakistan, Morocco, and Tunisia have all agreed to reduce pesticide and fertilizer subsidies substantially. Judicial use of both pesticides and chemical fertilizers has helped countries increase their crop yield on existing land substantially (Pakistan, Indonesia, and the Philippines), thereby limiting encroachment on forest lands. As already described, however, the excessive and indiscriminate use of pesticides encouraged by generous subsidies has proved counterproductive by eliminating the pests' natural predators or promoting the emergence of pesticide-resistant strains of pests. Similarly, overapplication of chemical fertilizers over a prolonged period of time, to the total exclusion of organic fertilizers (such as manure), damages the structure of the soil. Heavy use of pesticides and chemical fertilizers also leads to water pollution and poisoning of aquatic life through runoff into the water systems. It does not matter that chemical subsidies have been cut to reduce the drain on the budget; their reduction also reduces the drain on the environment. Ideally, however, environmentally destructive inputs (pesticides and chemical fertilizers) should be taxed in proportion to their negative externalities, and environmentally beneficial inputs (integrated pest management, organic fertilizers, and soil conservation) should be subsidized in proportion to their positive externalities. There is no such provision, however, in structural adjustment programs; any positive environmental effects are incidental rather than integral to these programs.

To the extent that structural adjustment programs require water pricing to improve efficiency in resource allocation or cost recovery to reduce budget deficits, water resources are conserved and environmental costs are reduced. Not only are salinization and waterlogging contained but, more important, the alleviation of water shortages through demand management also averts the environmental problems of constructing new irrigation systems.

Structural adjustment programs also call for reductions in subsidies (or import duty exemptions) for farm equipment and land-clearing machinery, again as part of their objective of reducing budget and trade deficits and eliminating policy-induced distortions. This policy reform has several positive effects on resource use and the state of the environment, because subsidized land-clearing machinery encourages deforestation and the clearing of marginal lands for agriculture, compacts and damages the structure of fragile tropical soils, increases the use of fossil fuels, and distorts the farmer's labor-capital choice in favor of capital and against labor in countries with abundant labor. Aside from the economic inefficiency and misallocation of scarce capital that the latter entails, it also reduces agricultural employment, thereby promoting encroachment on forest lands and undue urban migration.

Structural adjustment policies also require reduction of agricultural credit subsidies, as in the case of the Philippines and Tunisia. The impact of this measure is somewhat ambiguous. If credit subsidies are benefiting large farmers and ranchers engaged in large-scale land clearing (as is the case in Latin America more than in Asia or Africa), reducing these subsidies clearly reduces environmental degradation. If, on the other hand, credit subsidies are benefiting small farmers who have inadequate funds for intensification on existing lands and investment in land improvement and soil conservation, any reduction of these subsidies will induce more soil mining and forest land encroachment than is currently the case. Even in the case of the small farmer, however, there are superior policies to outright credit subsidies, which are in any case fungible and can be used for other purposes. Removal of interest rate ceilings, issue of secure land titles that can be used as collateral, and increased credit availability at competitive rates are better for the farmer, the budget, and the environment than credit subsidies, because they optimize the use of both capital and land. Credit subsidies are an incentive to borrow but not an incentive to invest in soil conservation or tree planting if the farmer does not have secure land ownership.

CHAPTER 4

Achieving Sustainable Development through Policy Reform

Virtually every developing country faces some degree of deforestation, watershed destruction, soil erosion, insecure land
use, excessive pesticide application, and inefficient water use.
Issues of more localized interest include shifting cultivation in
Southeast Asia, overgrazing in Africa and the Near East, waterlogging in South Asia (Pakistan) and the Near East (especially
Egypt), cattle ranching subsidies in Latin America (Brazil), and
desertification in the arid lands of India, the Middle East, and
Africa. Governments around the world are increasingly recognizing that this environmental degradation poses growing
threats to the sustainability of the growth process. In response
to these concerns, governments have changed existing policies
and introduced new policies and programs. Increasingly, policy successes, though still far fewer than policy failures, are
easier to find.

A policy success is a government intervention, or the elimination of one, that improves the allocation of resources and
reduces the degradation of the environment. Policy successes
can be classified into three groups: First is the reduction and
eventual elimination of policies (taxes, subsidies, quotas, and
public projects) that distort well-functioning markets or exacerbate market failures. The radical change in Indonesian policy

105

toward pesticides in recent years is a case in point. Following economic analysis that showed negative returns from insecticides and agroecological research that confirmed the link between insecticide use and the surge of brown planthopper that threatened 70 percent of Java's rice crop, a 1986 presidential decree banned fifty-seven registered brands of broad-spectrum insecticides, twenty of which were heavily subsidized by the government. The same decree established integrated pest management as the national pest control strategy for rice (see Case 8 on page 64 for details). Likewise, Brazil recently reduced or eliminated most of the credit subsidies and tax breaks for the conversion of natural forests in the Amazon to privately lucrative but socially unprofitable ranches (see Case 2 on page 14).

The second form of policy success is the correction or mitigation of market failures through interventions that improve the functioning of the market or result in outcomes superior to those of the free market. For instance, Singapore uses marginal cost pricing to control urban congestion (see Case 12 on page 92), while China has introduced water pricing to deal with water shortages (see Case 13 on page 112).

A third kind of policy success is the internalization of environmental, social, and other side effects of public projects and sectoral and macroeconomic policies. Examples include the Dumoga-Bone irrigation project and national park in Indonesia, which uses water pricing to improve irrigation efficiency and to fund the management of a watershed area that has been declared a national park (see Case 6 on page 28), and the inclusion of environmental provisions in several structural adjustment programs.

Other cases of policy success exist as well. Recently there has been a shift toward reducing subsidies in the Philippines, Pakistan, Tunisia, and Morocco. In many cases, the pressure comes more from a need to reduce the burden on the budget rather than the burden on the environment, although the latter is increasingly a factor as pesticide and fertilizer subsidies are considered in macroeconomic and trade policy reform discussions and negotiations for structural adjustment loans (SALs). Iona Sebastian and Adelaida Alicbusan report that the Philippines, Nepal, Morocco, and Tunisia have agreed to reduce their fertilizer subsidies as part of SAL packages.[1]

With regard to land ownership, Tunisia, Morocco, Nepal, and Thailand have recently accelerated their land titling programs to improve security of ownership (see Case 10 on page 72), while Papua New Guinea recognizes and protects customary communal tenure over land and forest resources (see Case 4 on page 20). Kenya has seen a resurgence of self-help groups that effectively manage community resources (see Case 14 on page 114).

Needed Policy Reforms

Policy reform is simply the restructuring of government interventions from areas of policy failure to areas of policy success (see Figure 2). The absolute level of government intervention may not change and may in fact decrease depending on the magnitude of market distortions to be eliminated relative to market failures to be corrected or mitigated.

This analysis of environmental degradation reveals the root causes of natural resource depletion and environmental degradation: policy distortions and market failures, and the corollary failure of underinvesting in human resource development and employment alternatives. These root causes also point toward the type of policy overhaul necessary to improve resource management and make the development process more sustainable. A comprehensive policy reform should have five components:

1. It should eliminate or at least reduce policy distortions that favor environmentally unsound practices at the same time as they discriminate against the poor, reduce economic efficiency, and waste budgetary resources.

2. It should correct or at least mitigate market failures such as externalities, insecurity of ownership, and absent or imperfect markets that result in overexploitation of resources, through a system of institutions, incentives, regulation, and fiscal measures.

3. It should include investment in human resource development and rural industry to provide alternative

FIGURE 2

Policy and Market Successes and Failures in Responding to Increasing Resource Scarcity and Environmental Degradation

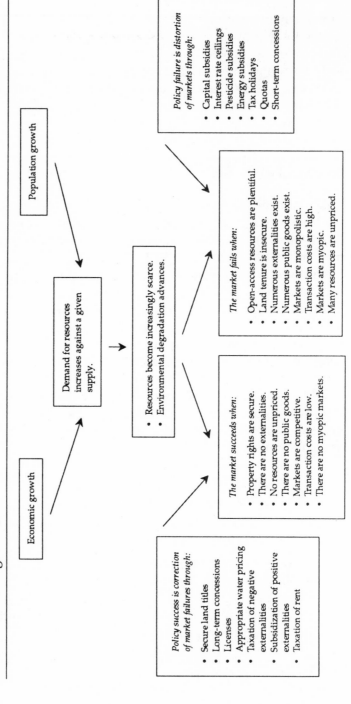

With market and policy success:

- Prices rise to reflect the increasing scarcity of resources.
- Waste is reduced.
- Efficiency improves.
- Substitution increases.
- Conservation efforts increase.
- Investment and technology develop new sources and new substitutes.

With market and policy failure:

- Prices (if they exist) do not respond to the increasing scarcity of resources.
- Wasteful use continues.
- Efficiency remains low.
- Available less harmful substitutes are not used.
- There are no incentives for conservation.
- There are no incentives for investment and technology to develop new substitutes.

Sustainable development:

- The economy grows.
- Poverty is reduced.
- Population growth slows down.
- Conservation takes place and the environment improves.
- Quality of life improves.

Unsustainable development:

- Economic growth slows.
- Poverty increases.
- Rapid population growth continues.
- Resources are depleted.
- The environment deteriorates.
- Quality of life falls.

SOURCE: Author.

employment to disadvantaged groups such as shifting cultivators, landless farmers, and underemployed workers, to lessen the pressure on natural resources and their use as a last resort activity.

4. It should apply broad social cost-benefit analysis to all public projects by: (a) casting them in the overall sectoral and macroeconomic policy context; (b) taking into account all benefits and costs, whether near or distant, whether economic, social, or environmental, and whether quantitative or qualitative; and (c) avoiding projects that lead to irreversible changes in the environment or foreclosure of options.

5. It should build analytical capability and institutional capacity for analyzing, formulating, and implementing policies and projects that have environmental dimensions.

This is a tall order and requires considerable political will, but movement in this direction is both necessary and feasible. It is necessary because the current situation is clearly untenable: not only are the current trends of resource depletion and environmental degradation unsustainable, but if they are continued they will undermine otherwise successful development strategies. Policy reform is feasible because the proposed policy reform would promote several national objectives with minimal trade-offs and budgetary costs: increased economic efficiency and growth, resource conservation and environmental protection, reductions in income inequalities, and, in some cases, savings in or additional sources of government revenues. The substantial policy reforms that have occurred in other areas such as taxation, the exchange rate, and general macroeconomic policy suggest that the political will for change does exist among policy makers.

The first priority is to eliminate, reduce, or cushion policies that have significant environmental costs or perverse incentives that encourage resource depletion and environmental degradation beyond the level that is even privately optimal. Unless these perverse incentives are removed, project investments aimed at improved use and conservation of natural resources are unlikely to succeed, and when they do, their impact will be unsustainable, lasting only as long as the project. Re-forming policies that are detrimental to both the economy and the environment is also the easiest place to start because no difficult development-environment trade-offs or budget out-lays are involved. If anything, eliminating policy distortions usually reduces budget outlays, in many cases reduces govern-ment expenditures, and may even generate additional budget revenues. The distributional implications are also positive since many of these distortions are sources of not only inefficiency and resource depletion, but also inequity. Finally, eliminating policy distortions can be done by adjusting prices, taxes, and subsidies, which is easier than introducing new instruments or developing new institutions to deal with market failures. Therefore, eliminating policy distortions is the place to start, but it is only a start, because without correction or at least mitigation of market failures, a country cannot achieve efficient use and conservation of resources.

The overall objective of policy reform is to reestablish the link between resource scarcity and resource prices that has been severed by a constellation of subsidies, perverse incen-tives, and unmitigated market and institutional failures such as insecure land tenure, open-access fisheries and forests, and unaccounted environmental externalities. Reestablishing the link between resource scarcity and resource prices is critical to improving resource management and sustainable develop-ment. Population growth, economic growth, and improvement in the quality of life are all increasing the demand for a dwin-dling supply of natural resources and environmental ameni-ties. This demand, if not reflected in higher resource prices or if cushioned through subsidies, will result in accelerated re-source depletion and environmental degradation, culminating in unsustainable development. If, on the other hand, the grow-ing resource scarcity is reflected in increasing resource prices, it will stimulate efforts to reduce the growth of demand through resource conservation, improved efficiency, and substitution and to expand supply through recycling, exploration, imports, and development of substitutes. It will also encourage struc-tural change in the use of natural resources, which will go from being sources of raw materials and dumpsites for waste disposal to being sources of environmental amenities and

CASE 13

Policy Success: Water Pricing in China

For centuries irrigation has played a crucial role in Chinese agriculture. Since the Communist Revolution in 1949, the area of irrigated land has tripled, and 75 percent of national food production is on irrigated land, contributing to China's food self-sufficiency.[1]

In July 1985, the People's Republic of China took an important first step toward promoting more efficient use of irrigation water, when the government instituted agricultural policy reforms giving provincial water management agencies greater financial and managerial autonomy. The reforms emphasized "water as a commodity rather than a gift of nature and clearly attributed wasteful consumption and the imbalance between supply and demand to irrationally low water charges."[2] As a result, irrigation water is priced more closely to its actual cost, and problems associated with overuse and inefficient distribution have diminished.

The budgets of the water management agencies now depend on irrigation service fees paid by water users and income generated by agency projects such as fishing and livestock production. Irrigation service fees are set at levels adequate to cover operation, maintenance, and amortization of capital costs. Beginning in 1980, the government switched from financing new irrigation systems with grants to providing loans. The move provided an extra incentive for water management agencies to collect higher water fees.

In general, water charges are determined by what the water actually costs for different uses. For example, charges may vary according to season, and in very dry areas progressive water pricing schemes have been adopted to reflect scarcity. Irrigation for grain crops is priced according to supply costs without profit, while cash crops may be irrigated for slightly higher than cost.

The reforms also serve to decentralize authority, giving water management agencies more responsibility for both the operation of irrigation facilities and the distribution of irrigation water. This decentralized management has led to more efficient distribution practices, such as distributing water according to land area, levying water charges on a volumetric basis rather than a flat rate, and preparing distribution plans in advance. In Hungxian County, farmers reported that they had a more reliable water supply and were willing to pay more for the guaranteed supply.[3] Management is often further decentralized when a local agency purchases water wholesale and sells it in bulk to smaller water-user associations responsible for distribution to farmers. These smaller groups strengthen the bond between the water user and the supplier who must recover costs.

Because of these policy reforms, revenues collected by the water management agencies have increased significantly. Farmers have begun to irrigate their crops more efficiently, using less water per hectare.[4] At the same time, crop production has improved, with China producing twice as much as similarly irrigated crops in India.[5]

---

1. Asian Development Bank (ADB) and International Irrigation Management Institute, *Irrigation Service Fees*, Proceedings of the Regional Seminar on Irrigation Service Fees (Manila: ADB, 1986).

2. Lester Ross, *Environmental Policy in China* (Bloomington: Indiana University Press, 1988).

3. Asian Development Bank and International Irrigation Management Institute, *Irrigation Service Fees*.

4. Ibid.

5. Peter Rogers, "Fresh Water," in Robert Repetto, ed., *The Global Possible: Resources, Development, and the New Century* (New Haven: Yale University Press, 1985).

CASE 14

Policy Success:
Community Self-Help Groups in Katheka, Kenya

Since the early 1980s, volunteer self-help groups in the Kenyan village of Katheka have contributed significantly to controlling soil erosion, improving water catchment, and increasing food production. Fifteen volunteer groups, including twelve women's groups, meet twice weekly to work on a group member's farm and to carry out community projects.[1] Projects, which are often self-funded, have included terracing land, digging cut-off drains, and installing check dams.

In 1973 soil erosion had reached nearly intolerable levels in Katheka, which has an annual rainfall of 400–600 millimeters. Tree removal was rampant, and soil conservation efforts were nonexistent. Voluntary women's groups known as *mwethya*, or self-help groups, had been organized for centuries in times of need. During colonial times, however, the tradition had all but disappeared. For unknown reasons, the *mwethya* witnessed a resurgence in the mid-1970s. Within a few years the groups, which were predominantly women, were actively working and results were beginning to show.[2]

The *mwethya* have led to increased environmental awareness among women. Respondents to a village survey almost unanimously commented that soil conservation increases water retention and consequently food production. They also agreed that terracing is critical to sustaining and increasing yields. This awareness leads to more efficient farming practices and sustainable food production.

Decision making and implementation are the responsibility solely of the groups. As a result the women are invested with a strong sense of leadership and responsibility. It is they who benefit from the more efficient practices they choose to adopt. The groups are organized with incentives for participation. If, for example, a member misses two or three work sessions, the group skips over that person's farm during the course of the rotation.

While Katheka residents have practiced effective resource management within the confines of the *mwethya*, they do not have the management capabilities or access to economic resources to combat external forces. Indeed, whenever external forces do become involved, trouble seems to arise. For example, Nairobi businesses often send trucks to dig sand from the dry riverbeds. As a result of the sand removal, less water can be stored for the dry season. Dams built by the *mwethya* are rendered useless, and the riverbed lining is removed, increasing the rate of water flow during rainstorms and raising the rate of soil being carried away.

Despite these problems, the *mwethya* of Katheka remain mobilized to institute effective resource management. When such groups are invested with the ultimate responsibility for success or failure, the results are often positive. As farmers witness sustainable increased yields due to more efficient practices, they learn the value of resource management and conservation.

---

1. Material for this case comes from Program for International Development, Clark University, in cooperation with National Environment Secretariat, Ministry of Environment and Natural Resources, Government of Kenya, *Resources, Management Population and Local Institutions in Katheka: A Case Study of Effective Natural Resources Management in Machakos, Kenya* (Worcester, Mass.: Clark University, 1988).

2. As of July 1987 there were fifteen groups with 400 members, all but 40 of whom were women.

improved quality of life, consistent with growing incomes and expanding material wealth. These very responses to growing resource prices would result in both economic growth and environmental conservation through more efficient resource use, increased substitution of lower-cost, more abundant sources of supply, increased investment in human capital, and technological development.

Forest Policy Reforms

Log export bans and logging bans are well-intentioned responses to the need to increase value added from a depletable resource (Indonesia), to the growing scarcity of forest resources (Philippines), and to ecological disasters (Thailand), but they often accomplish the reverse of the intended result. The reason is simple. These policies depress rather than increase the value of the resource, thereby inducing more waste and less conservation. Making a resource less valuable is usually not an effective way of saving it. What is needed is a reform of current forest policies to encourage efficient harvesting and processing and to promote investments in forest regeneration and conservation.

A forest policy reform might include the following elements, most of which can be done by developing countries themselves without outside interference and with minimal external support:

1. Reclassify forest lands into land disposable to individuals, land disposable to groups of individuals or communities, and nondisposable land over which the state retains ownership and control. The criterion for this classification should be the extent of externalities in terms of both intensity and spatial distribution. Forest lands with no significant externalities can be safely distributed and securely titled to the dispossessed, such as landless farmers, chronically idle laborers, and shifting cultivators. Forest lands with localized externalities, such as local watersheds, can be made communal property, provided that a community small and cohesive enough to manage them

effectively can be defined. And forest lands with regional or national externalities such as major watersheds or nature reserves should stay under state ownership, which would probably be most effective over a limited area with reduced outside pressure. (India has been experimenting with assigning responsibility for forest lands to small user groups; see Case 15 on page 118.)

2. Change the procedure for awarding concessions, from negotiations with the concessionaires and licensing with nominal fees to competitive bidding. This will maximize the government's share of the resource rents, help keep logging out of marginal lands, and reduce the perceived risk of renegotiation of concession agreements. Concessionaires should be provided with financial instruments for accumulating equity through forest investments that are transferable and marketable, to encourage them to invest in conservation and reforestation.

3. Increase the duration and scope of the exploitation leases sufficiently to encourage production of nontimber forest products and services and forest regeneration for subsequent felling cycles.

4. Protect the concession area from encroachment, and enforce the terms of the concession agreement.

5. Reform the tax system to eliminate incentives for destructive logging. For example, change the tax base from the volume of timber removed to the volume of merchantable timber on the site to eliminate the incentive for high grading and forest mining.

6. Determine whether any harvesting of timber, fuelwood, and nontimber goods should be allowed in protective forests. If so, specify the areas, set the conditions and restrictions, define who should be allowed to harvest, and devise an enforceable cost-effective system of incentives and penalties that would regulate access and use without unacceptable trade-offs between the primary protective function and the secondary productive function. This would require research and experimentation in assessing

CASE 15

Experimenting with Communal Resource Management:
The Arabari Experiment in India

India's Arabari experiment began in West Bengal in 1970 as a response to the rapid deforestation in that region. The objective of the experiment was to find out how to stop villagers from encroaching on the forest for illegal firewood. Interviews with thirteen hundred people in eleven villages revealed the villagers were earning much of their income from the illegal cutting and selling of firewood.

The experiment offered the villagers forest-related employment opportunities from which they could earn at least as much as they earned from forest encroachment. The villagers were employed in planting trees and grass on blank patches. Planting was scheduled to take place during the low-employment season. The government arranged for outside sources to provide fuelwood and construction poles to the villagers at cost. In addition, through a revenue-sharing agreement with the Forest Department, the villagers received 25 percent of the selling price of mature trees in cash. The villagers were also entrusted with the responsibility of protecting the forest from encroachment. Institutional arrangements were made for the election of representatives from among the villagers to monitor the work and to collect and distribute payments.

Following these changes the villagers enforced total protection of the forest, and they themselves refrained from illegal cutting. They imposed and enforced a reduction of firewood cutting and introduced watching and patrolling by villagers. After fifteen years, the degraded forests were rehabilitated, the villagers were markedly better off, and their relations with the Forest Department improved. Gradually the experiment was expanded to more villages, and by 1989 there were more than 700 groups or Village Protection Committees, protecting more than 70,000 hectares of degraded lands that were planted to forests in West Bengal. "The will to do so developed as these groups believed in the assurance of sustained benefits."[1] Similar success with small user groups has been reported in Nepal, Indonesia, and Niger.

These success stories show that for collective action to succeed the following conditions must be met:

1. A link must be created between a well-defined small group and a well-defined piece of forest land.

2. The group members must perceive a clear correlation between their contributions and their returns.

3. Both authority and benefits flowing from resource management must be restricted to members of the group to the exclusion of outsiders and free riders.[2]

4. The degree of group cooperation must be established according to the particular communities' degree of social cohesion and experience with collective action.

---

1. A. K. Banerjee, "A Case of Group Formation in Forest Management" (June 1989), mimeo.

2. Michael M. Cernea, "User Groups as Producers in Participatory Afforestation Strategies," Development Discussion Paper No. 319 (Cambridge, Mass.: Harvard Institute for International Development, 1989).

trade-offs between competing uses, predicting behavior in response to penalties and incentives, and evaluating the cost-effectiveness of alternative policy instruments.

7. Invest in the protection, management, and enhancement of the state-owned productive forests based on strict criteria of social profitability.

8. Devise an enforceable, cost-effective, and efficient system of laws and institutions to stimulate innovative approaches to the protection and management of national parks and biological reserves set aside for the conservation of genetic resources and the preservation of wilderness and recreation values.

9. Promote private forest investments through an appropriate incentive structure and financial mechanisms, such as cofinancing of long-term loans; longer grace, disbursement, and repayment periods; establishment of guarantee funds to reduce risk; and insurance against pest outbreaks and forest fires.

10. With regard to public benefits generated by private forest investments, such as downstream irrigation benefits, provide commensurate incentives such as tax exemptions and subsidies linked to these benefits to bring forest investments to a level consistent with long-term economic and social profitability. For instance, the tax structure should favor natural forest management over plantations, mixed-species plantations over single-species plantations, and single-species plantations over erosive crops such as corn and cassava. Eucalyptus and pine plantations should be taxed or promoted in proportion to their net social and environmental effects on the water table, soil erosion, and nutrient depletion. Logging companies could be provided with incentives to set aside part of their concessions as nature reserves (for conservation purposes) and extractive reserves for the extraction of nontimber forest products by local communities and to manage the rest on a sustainable basis.

11. Recognize and accommodate the customary rights of access to and use of forests by local communities. Their

physical presence in the forest and their intimate knowledge of the local ecology can be of immense value in the protection and regeneration of the forest and the harvesting and use of nontimber products.

These reforms should be strongly supported by both commercial forestry (producers and consumers) and developing country governments, because they will ensure sustainable supplies of tropical hardwoods and will transform tropical commercial forestry from an extractive industry into a sustainable economic activity with considerable private and social net benefits. Although higher hardwood prices may be perceived as running against the short-term interests of commercial forestry (especially by the importers and consumers), the long-term benefits appropriately discounted exceed any short-term costs. Unless consumers pay higher prices for tropical hardwoods, there can be no conservation, and without conservation there can be no sustainable supplies. Currently, the waste, inefficiency, and damage to regeneration are so great that it is possible, by instituting these reforms, to make every party involved better off. Alternatives such as export bans, logging bans, import bans, or other similar prohibitions or trade restrictions are misguided and counterproductive, as the experience of countries such as Thailand, Indonesia, and the Philippines demonstrates.

Policies to Conserve Biological Diversity

Any reduction in natural forests inevitably leads to some extinction, or some attrition of genetic diversity. The aim of conservation must therefore be to optimize, rather than to preserve everything, which in practice is impossible. Specialized animals and plants can, as a rule, survive in relatively small areas that are maintained in a completely unexploited, unmodified state. Generalized species often require larger areas, but cyclical selective exploitation is not usually harmful to them.

A system of carefully selected preserves with a minimum individual size for each habitat of at least 5,000 hectares, connected with corridors of managed natural forest, which together make up a total conservation area of at least 100,000 hectares, may suffice in many cases to preserve the great majority of both specialized and generalized species. The preserves would, of course, have to be environmentally heterogeneous to ensure adequate representation of genetic resources. In principle, a few large environmentally heterogeneous preserves are preferable to many small environmentally uniform preserves and have the added advantage of preserving wilderness and aesthetic values. Selectively logged corridors connecting strict preserves must be managed so that keystone food plants such as figs are preserved.[2] Finally, the full range of sites in each climatic zone must have adequate representation of the zone's genetic resources, with highest priority given to areas with a concentration of endemic species and with a diverse range of species.[3]

The above principles would help determine the minimum size necessary to maintain biological diversity in a tropical forest. For ecological and social reasons, however, the size of the reserve may not be stable or sustainable. Preliminary results of experiments in Brazil show that the "the smallest plots gradually become overrun by encroaching growth, usually by a single species of tree, lending credence to the idea of having buffer zones surrounding parks of pristine forest."[4]

Setting up nature reserves and buffer zones, whatever the ecological and social justification, is costly. First, there is the opportunity cost of the forest and land resources that are taken out of intensive use; this cost is roughly the forgone value of timber and crops that could be produced in the absence of the reserve and its buffer zone. Then there is the cost of identifying, demarcating, protecting, and managing the area to be conserved (core reserve). Finally, there is the cost of issuing and enforcing communal or private rights over the buffer zone and providing adequate incentives for sustainable resource use.

The substantial cost involved in setting up reserves raises three questions: First, what is the socially optimal level of biological conservation? That is, how much should a country invest in setting up nature reserves and buffer zones and designing appropriate incentives and enforcement mechanisms? Second, what form should the incentives, monitoring, and enforcement take? Third, how can the government or other local authorities and communities generate revenues from nature reserves to pay for protection, monitoring, and management of the reserves?

Answering these questions requires research beyond the scope of this book. Nevertheless, some guidelines for both policy and research can be given here. With regard to the first question, the government should be prepared to spend an amount up to the total social benefit derived from conservation, which includes a variety of use values such as scientific, educational, aesthetic, recreational, medicinal, climatic, hydraulic, and commercial values. In addition to these use values, there are nonuse values. For instance, people derive pleasure (or utility) simply from knowing that a resource with unique characteristics exists, even though they have no plans to use it in any way. People also often prefer to keep their options open to use a resource at some point in the future, if they so desire, although they have no such plans now. Resources have a bequest value because people derive pleasure from passing on to their children part of the natural environment that they themselves have inherited from previous generations. Finally, certain cultures and religions place value on preserving the natural environment.

Experience shows that reserve forests and national parks are constantly encroached upon by surrounding populations in search of land, food, fuelwood, and building materials, as well as by illegal loggers. Buffer zones between areas of intensive land use (logging or farming) and areas of strict conservation may help control encroachment if they offer employment opportunities that are more attractive than encroachment. For example, the buffer zones may be exploited for nontimber goods on a sustainable basis or developed into areas for recreation and tourism. For these buffer zones to be effective, the people living in the forest or its perimeter (squatters and shifting cultivators) should benefit from the new activities, and the open-access status of the buffer zones should be terminated to prevent new entrants from dissipating any benefits that the buffer zones would generate.

The most cost-effective means of meeting both conditions is likely to be the granting of secure and exclusive territorial rights over the buffer zone to the local communities that currently

depend on the forest for their livelihood. Such communal property rights are analogous to those in effect in Papua New
Guinea (see Case 4 on page 20). As long as the incentive structure is designed to favor sustainable use over logging and
slash-and-burn farming, and the property rights are allocated
to communities with a functioning social organization, self-
enforcement can be relied on to protect the buffer zone and the
core area of the reserve from encroachment. When a large number of communities is involved, however, a higher local authority or the government may need to play a more active role in
enforcing communal rights, arbitrating conflicts between communities, and providing additional protection to the core nature reserve.

Although all these use and nonuse values are known to
exist and to vary depending on the type of resource and the
population concerned, assigning a dollar value to them is not
an easy task. It is, however, by no means impossible. In recent
years, researchers have developed methods for valuing commodities and services that are not exchanged in the market.
There are three categories of such methods: (1) those that as-
sign value from observable market behavior (such as the travel
cost method), (2) those that attempt to imitate market valuation
by creating surrogate markets, and (3) those that solicit a direct
valuation from the relevant population (the contingent valuation method). The purpose of all these methods is to derive a
proximate estimate of people's willingness to pay for biological
conservation.

Since biological conservation is an international public
good, the relevant population is not limited to the local or
national population but includes the rest of the world as well,
especially people living in the developed countries. These people are the main consumers of biological conservation, through
scientific and recreational tourism and medical research, and of
environmental amenities, including conservation for its own
sake. This is not to say that the local populations derive no
benefits. But given their low level of income, their main benefit
comes from their ability to convert biological conservation into
direct economic benefits such as the harvesting of nontimber
goods, employment as forest guards or tour guides, access fees

for scientists and tourists, and a secure and stable water supply from watershed protection.

This raises questions about the appropriate form of conservation incentives for local populations and mechanisms for cost recovery. Indonesia's experience with the Dumoga-Bone irrigation–national park project and India's experience with economic incentives for rural communities adjacent to wildlife reserves are relevant in this respect.[5] Another example comes from Costa Rica, which has successfully used a number of innovative instruments such as charges for scientists carrying out research in tropical forests and leasing of prospecting rights for new substances to pharmaceutical companies. It has also promoted nature-oriented tourism. Brazil, following protests by traditional rubber tappers over the destruction of their sources of livelihood, has established extractive reserves for sustainable harvesting of nontimber products by indigenous people. It is too early to assess the success of this scheme, however, which met with considerable opposition from conflicting interests.

Water Policy Reforms

A reform in water management policies must overhaul irrigation policy to provide incentives for efficient water use, to increase cost recovery, and to generate funds for rehabilitation, maintenance, and improvement of existing irrigation systems. The first steps in such a reform should be to strengthen water-user associations and to make structural modifications to existing irrigation systems, such as intermediate storage at the head of distribution channels and installation of meters in secondary channels. Such modifications would make possible "bulk water sales through contract with water-user associations and cooperatives as irrigation agencies do in Mexico, India, China and other countries."[6] Other steps would be to develop cost-recovery mechanisms, such as user charges indexed to factors like the value of crops, land taxes, water rights, and provisions for water trading, which would encourage farmers to value water at its marginal opportunity cost.

Bulk water sales to water-user associations could help reduce metering and collection costs by leaving water distribution to local organizations, which can best monitor water use and prevent meter manipulation or damage through peer group pressure. Robert Repetto reports that "in Gujarat State in India, the irrigation agency sells water volumetrically in bulk to cooperatives, which distribute and collect fees from their members."[7] A similar system operates in Sri Lanka. Lester Ross reports that the introduction of volumetric irrigation fees in areas of China has induced farmers to use water more efficiently and has generated revenues for maintenance of the irrigation systems (see Case 13 on page 112).[8]

When volumetric (marginal cost) pricing is not feasible or prohibitively costly, low-cost approximations such as area-based irrigation charges and land taxes could be introduced. The sacrifice of efficiency in this case may be justified by the savings in metering and collection costs. The evidence worldwide suggests that farmers are prepared to pay for reliable irrigation services. Availability and reliability of supply is far more important to them than cost.

The same principles that apply to irrigation water should apply to all other uses of water, including industry, energy, and household use. Water consumers in all sectors in most developing (and many developed) countries pay a flat charge for water, which is well below the real cost of delivery, let alone its opportunity cost or scarcity value. Thus consumers are encouraged and in many cases explicitly subsidized to overuse and waste water, often on account of "equity": water is too essential to deprive the poor of its use through pricing. Yet both equity and efficiency objectives could be served by progressive water charges that reflect long-run supply costs. In fact, the current system is inequitable because it taxes the general public, including the poor (who as wage earners often bear a disproportionate tax burden because of their inability to evade it), to subsidize wasteful water uses by the wealthy (such as large lawns and gardens).

Water is also demanded for use as a receptacle for waste water by industry, municipalities, and households. In many countries this use of water for waste disposal is free, and, as one would expect, water resources near industries, urban centers, and tourist towns become overpolluted and degraded. In other countries, especially those at a higher level of development, waste disposal in water resources is regulated by permit, by requirements for water treatment before disposal, or by effluent standards. However, compliance is poorly monitored, the penalties are too low, and they are not strictly enforced. Such standards and regulations often work better as incentives for consumers to engage in rent-seeking behavior than as regulation of waste disposal. Again, water pricing for waste disposal is a more effective instrument because it manages demand and suggests to users alternatives that are less costly than bribing enforcement officials, such as switching to less-polluting inputs and technologies, installing treatment facilities, or changing location.

In conclusion, water users should pay fully for the costs of supply, delivery, depletion, and pollution treatment attributable to their use. The payment should be linked to the quantity and quality of use, and the link should be transparent enough to channel the user's efforts toward efficient use, conservation, and minimization of waste generation and disposal. As long as there is a divergence between those who use (agriculture, industry, households) and those who pay (taxpayers), there is no built-in conservation mechanism. If there is such a mechanism, it is a perverse one because it encourages internalization of the benefits from water use and externalization of the costs. The government, in its attempt to correct one market failure, has generated another.

Urban and Industrial Policy Reforms

The causes of environmental problems have been described as massive market failures and policy distortions. Environmental resources such as air, water, landscape, and atmosphere are common property, unpriced resources outside the domain of markets. While the use of other resources such as capital and labor is subject to prices and other constraints, the use of environmental resources is not. Urban consumers and industrial producers dump raw wastes into the air and water without regard to the high costs they impose on others and the society at large, precisely because it is economically advantageous for them to do so. Waste disposal is free; waste reduction or treatment is costly.

If environmental resources could be brought into the market and priced, their prices would indicate their true scarcity and the opportunity costs of their use. Users would have to pay to use environmental resources, and such payments would force them to economize on their use. The entire spectrum of industrial decisions would be affected: the design of industrial processes and technologies, the types and quantities of raw materials used, and the nature of products produced. Therefore, the ideal solution would be to establish a market for environmental resources by defining property rights by governmental action, since transaction costs prevent the spontaneous emergence of such a market. Pollution rights (or pollution permits) could be issued and allocated to current industrial producers in a "grandfather system" that makes it easier for existing firms to comply. Pollution permits could be either bought back by the government or gradually reduced in value (that is, the level of allowable pollution) until the desirable level of environmental quality is reached. Pollution permits should be marketable and transferable so that they will gravitate to the most efficient producers and their prices will reflect the true scarcity of environmental resources being used.

Despite its many merits, a system of pollution permits has not yet been extensively used anywhere, and its details have not been fully worked out. The concept of marketable pollution permits is a relatively recent idea that is currently being tried in the United States on an experimental basis. What I propose here is research into the feasibility of such a system in developing countries. In fact, it might be easier to introduce such a system into a country that is not yet fully industrialized. In industrialized countries, vested interests, sunk investments, and damage already done militate against pollution permits.

Some countries, however, have had success with alternatives that approximate the workings of a market for environmental resources. Instead of relying on the market to set prices for environmental resources, the government sets charges for the use of these resources through legislative or executive decision. If these charges are properly set, the external costs will be internalized and environmental resources will be optimally used.

Ideally, charges for destructive uses of the environment

such as disposal of wastes should be set equal to the damage or external costs that these activities generate. In practice, it is very difficult to estimate the full extent of environmental damage because it is widespread and difficult to quantify, and it takes a long time to accumulate. A more workable system of setting charges is one based on ambient standards. This is done in two stages. First, technical experts describe the consequences of different levels of ambient quality: for example, fish survival at different levels of dissolved oxygen or human health at different levels of carbon monoxide. Then, a target level of ambient quality (for example, a target level of dissolved oxygen or a maximum acceptable level of carbon monoxide) is politically or administratively chosen, and a charge for emissions is set at the level necessary to attain this target. The level of the charge for each area that would accomplish the target level of air or water quality is obtained by estimating the relationship between different charge levels and the emissions from different sources based on the average marginal costs of these sources. The effect of different levels of emissions on ambient quality can be determined through mathematical models of river basins or air pollution regions. These two relationships (between charges and emissions and between emissions and ambient quality) provide the link between charges and ambient quality and determine the level of the charges that will bring about the target level of ambient quality.

A system of charges, thus designed, will not result in polluters' paying a price equal to the external costs or damages created by their activities, unless the charges vary according to the location of the source of pollution. Such fine-tuning may prove to be prohibitively costly. Even in its crudest form, however, a system of pollution charges has advantages over the current system of direct regulation through effluent or ambient standards.

Emission charges are efficient means for achieving the desired level of environmental quality because they minimize the costs of pollution control by leaving the level of individual pollution control and the choice of technology to the polluter. Depending on his own control costs, a polluter faced with a charge on emissions may choose to reduce his output, change his input mix or production process, treat the waste, or simply pay the charge. Industries with high control costs would control less and pay more in charges, while industries with low control costs would control more and pay less in charges. Overall, the desired reduction in pollution will be attained at the minimum cost, and the industry will be under constant pressure to develop more cost-efficient ways of reducing or abating pollution in order to reduce its control costs or payment of charges. Enforcement is easier and simpler because charges require no knowledge of the production and abatement technologies of different industries and no bargaining; the incentive structure facing the polluter is such that it promotes self-enforcement. The onus of finding or developing the most efficient approach to reduction of emissions is on the polluters themselves, not on the regulatory agency.

The system of pollution charges has been used with considerable success in several countries. Japan has instituted a system of air and water charges to compensate the victims of pollution-related ailments. The Japanese compensation program uses statistics and epidemiology to allocate social responsibility for ailments to specific toxic substances. For example, sulfur oxides have been linked to respiratory diseases, and the compensation cost was allocated 20 percent to automobiles (to be paid out of an automobile tax) and 80 percent to all other sources of airborne sulfur oxides. The automobile tax varies according to car weight, and the charge on industry varies according to location in relation to the pollution zone. If an industry is identified as the only source of a particular toxic substance in the area, it is held responsible for all the compensation costs related to that substance regardless of the level of emissions. It is important to note that the national industrial association participated in the structuring of the program and its implementation, thus minimizing monitoring and collection costs.[9]

Variants of emission and effluent charges have been implemented with varying success in several countries. In the United States, towns receiving federal grants for construction of sewer systems are required by the Water Pollution Control Act to recover their operating costs and parts of the capital costs from their users, through municipal sewage treatment user charges. In the former West Germany, the private association of dischargers into the Ruhr Valley has levied charges on its members in proportion to their discharge levels and toxicity in order to finance collective control measures. Again, the process works smoothly because the charges are levied and collected by the representatives of the dischargers, not by the government. There is no reason why a system similar to the Japanese and the German ones cannot work in developing countries with appropriate industry leadership and some government encouragement.

Charge systems are also found in Eastern Europe. The former East Germany established emission charges for more than 100 different air pollutants. Anyone whose emissions were above the national standard paid the charge, and the proceeds were used to invest in environmental improvement and to compensate pollution victims. Similarly, Czechoslovakia and Poland instituted effluent charges on biological oxygen demand and suspended solids to attain a predetermined level of water quality. While impressive on paper, the East European economic incentive systems established under central planning failed to improve environmental conditions because of the soft budget constraint facing enterprises.

A comprehensive review of the application of pollution charges is beyond the scope of this book, but a few more examples that are potentially applicable to developing countries might be useful. These include a lead additive tax; a beverage container deposit; a recycling incentive tax; and product disposal, congestion, and noise charges. The U.S. government taxes leaded gasoline to reduce its price advantage over unleaded gasoline in order to induce a shift to the latter, which is less polluting. Many states in the United States have instituted refundable deposits on beverage and beer containers to discourage their free disposal and encourage their collection and recycling. Singapore, London, and Los Angeles use congestion charges during rush hours to reduce congestion and air pollution in the city center (see Case 12 on page 92), while Japan and the Netherlands have been considering noise charges for traffic and airport noise control.

It might be worthwhile for other countries to develop their own variants of pollution charges based on their special circumstances and enforcement difficulties. For example, beverage container deposits are likely to be effective in developing countries; even if they do not fully halt free disposal of wastes, they would stimulate the establishment of a new labor-intensive activity—the collection of containers and beer bottles—to use some of the abundant low-cost labor present in many developing countries.

CHAPTER 5

The Role of
Development Assistance

To reverse environmental degradation and achieve sustainable development, policy reform is indispensable. Yet policy reform, especially in the area of natural resources and the environment, is not an easy task. The vested interests created by existing policies are a major obstacle to change. In addition, long-term problems are overshadowed by pressing day-to-day issues. The need for reform is neither apparent nor pressing. Consensus for policy change emerges only at times of crisis, as exemplified by Thailand's introduction of a nationwide logging ban following catastrophic landslides and floods attributed to deforestation.

To respond before a crisis by developing long-term policies for ongoing management of natural resources is clearly more desirable. To do so, developing countries must build consensus and develop the capacity to research, formulate, and advance policy options that will lead to the efficient management of resources. Waiting for a major environmental crisis to attain consensus would be disastrous for the resource base and have possibly irreversible effects. Pushing forward with an outright policy reform would be equally disastrous in sociopolitical terms and could cause a backlash against similar efforts for years.

External concern, while useful and legitimate, cannot by itself bring policy reform. Pressure or conditionality imposed

by aid organizations is rarely well-received and is often counterproductive. Already, the eight Amazon nations have de-
nounced efforts by groups outside the region to dictate policies
concerning the use and management of the rain forests. Policy
change is not effective and sustainable unless understood, es-
poused, and promoted indigenously. Ultimately each country
needs to be able to determine the optimal use of its own forest
resources.

Foreign assistance is most effective when it aims to create
indigenous demand for and capacity to implement policy
change rather than to supply policy prescriptions. The most
acceptable and ultimately most useful way for aid agencies like
the World Bank and the U.S. Agency for International Development to effect policy reform is to create a conducive environment for and assist in the process of change. This can be
done with limited resources in a few targeted areas.

Although the priorities will vary according to each country's level of development, resource endowment, critical environmental problems, and existing capability for doing policy
analysis, I can recommend several general actions. Aid agencies should develop human resources in environmental management and policy sciences, with particular emphasis on natural resource economics and applied ecology. They should
initiate policy dialogue with policy makers on current and
emerging problems of natural resource management. They
should support research and policy analysis in natural resource
management through research grants and institutional development assistance to government agencies, universities, and
nongovernmental organizations (NGOs) concerned with resource management. They should strategically target projects
on natural resource management. They should offer technical
assistance in natural resource management. Finally, they
should disseminate information on the state, management,
and potential of natural resources and their role in sustainable
economic development and the quality of life. Such information will increase awareness and promote acceptance of the
need for changes in private behavior and public policy.

Success at carrying out these actions is the intermediate or
proximate objective, but the ultimate objective of these strategic
activities is to build consensus and capacity for policy change

that will improve the management of natural resources and the environment and, thereby, ensure the sustainability of the development process.

The strategic instruments may be grouped into five interconnected, partially overlapping, and mutually reinforcing groups: (1) policy dialogue; (2) pilot projects, institutional support, and technical assistance; (3) research support; (4) environmental awareness activities; and (5) education and training. These instruments are self-explanatory, except for the pilot policy projects and the policy workshops, which constitute the closest and most apparent link between projects and policies. As indicated earlier, one of the obstacles to policy change is the lack of an analytical basis for formulating alternative policies. For example, a government cannot predict the consequences of privatization of forest lands or the establishment of communal ownership in a buffer zone around a national park. We have *a priori* hypotheses based on theory and experience in various countries, but these hypotheses have not been tested in the countries concerned. It is far more difficult to effect a policy change when its consequences are unknown or highly uncertain.

The pilot policy projects would provide a testing ground for policy options. For example, with the support of local authorities, communal ownership of an estuary with a multiplicity of resources (fisheries, aquaculture potential, mangrove forest, tourism) could be introduced near a community known to have a cohesive social organization. Such a pilot project could be reinforced with support for social science research and observation/study tours in countries such as Sri Lanka and Japan, which have a long history of successful communal property systems. The results of such pilot projects could be used to make improvements and to replicate them in other sites with increased local participation. If successful, the knowledge and publicity generated from such experiments would encourage their extension to the national level.

Policy workshops (combined with research grants and the development of case studies) can aim at harnessing and enhancing existing analytical capacity and intellectual leadership in order to accelerate the process of environmentally critical policy reform. While it is true that developing countries lack sufficient analytical capacity in the specialized area of natural resource management and policy analysis, they have no lack of well-trained natural and social scientists and intellectual leaders. It is both feasible and cost-effective for aid organizations to harness existing analytical capacity by helping the best in-country talent become involved in applied research, seminars, and workshops on critical issues that can be dealt with in the relatively near term within existing constraints. This is essential for demonstrating the value of policy reform, gathering momentum, sustaining interest, and building a constituency for policy reform.

Local intellectual and political leaders must understand policy reform to be in their constituencies' best interests and must be able to defend it as such. The predominant view of environmental issues as luxuries of concern to the affluent developed countries must be replaced by accurate and informed discussions of their importance for the economic well-being, quality of life, and future of the local people themselves.

The performance of such a strategy and its individual projects and instruments can be evaluated at two levels: at the level of the intermediate or proximate objectives and at the level of the ultimate objective: the inducement of a policy change that would improve resource management. Evaluating performance at the intermediate (policy input) level is easier but less satisfactory than at the final (policy output) level. For example, human resource development or training can be evaluated based on the number of persons who have successfully completed training; this is an easier but less satisfactory evaluation than one based on the policy changes effected by those who have participated in the training. Similarly, research support may be evaluated based on the number and quality of research reports and publications, but more pertinent would be an evaluation of the impact of supported research on policy.

Aid agencies can monitor and evaluate the contribution of the strategy to information and knowledge based on the number and quality of research reports, publications, and statistical data banks, as well as the number of successfully completed pilot policy projects and the circulation of publications and journals established in connection with the strategy. They may judge the contribution to awareness and acceptance by polling a cross-section of the public or by observing a number of related indicators such as the trend in press coverage of environmental issues; the references to environmental issues in public statements by government officials, politicians, and business-people; public reaction to development projects with environmental implications; and the acknowledged consideration of environment-development trade-offs in policy decisions.

The strategy's performance in terms of enhancement of analytical capacity and experience may be evaluated in terms of the number of trainees that have successfully completed training; the number of pilot projects and study tours; the amount and quality of research completed; and the degree of competition for research grants. Finally, the strategy's contribution to institutional strength and commitment can be inferred from budget allocations to environment-related projects, especially by government agencies and NGOs supported by the project; new projects introduced by government agencies and NGOs patterned after the strategy; the number of government scholarships earmarked for environment-related training; the number of environment-related bills submitted to the legislature; and the level of borrowing by governments for natural resource–related projects.

Recognizing that success in intermediate objectives (policy inputs) may not necessarily be translated into policy changes (policy outputs), aid agencies should monitor and evaluate the strategy in terms of its impact on policy formulation as well. While it would be difficult to attribute or even link policy changes directly to the strategy, since some policy changes would have taken place anyway, it is possible to infer the contribution of the strategy by observing the speed and ease of policy change in areas where the strategy has supported projects, workshops, study tours, conferences, policy research, and training compared with other areas where the strategy had minimal involvement. Because of the slowness and incremental nature of policy change, the indicators for monitoring and evaluating the strategy's policy impact must be cast in terms of "movement in the right direction" or "progress toward" rather than "reversal of policies" or major "new initiatives." Here are some examples:

- progress toward issuing secure and transferable land titles to insecurely held land

- progress toward reform of the current concession and forest taxation systems (longer, competitively awarded concessions and simpler but higher taxation of rents are indicators of improvement)

- increasing recognition of the importance of nontimber forest products and services, assessment of their value, and introduction of policies that favor multiple-use management of tropical forests

- increased public investment allocations to rehabilitation and protection of critical watersheds

- progress toward the establishment of water-user associations, water rights, and water pricing

- reduction of agricultural taxation; elimination of agricultural chemical subsidies; and promotion of tree crops, ecologically sound farming systems, and integrated pest management

- movement toward recognition, rejuvenation, and strengthening of communal property rights as a cost-effective means of managing coastal resources, village forests, and buffer zones around national parks

- progress toward introduction of economic instruments such as pollution charges to replace or at least supplement the ineffective emission standards currently in use

- experimentation with refundable deposits for beverage containers and packaging material and with disposal charges and recycling incentives

- legislation requiring environmental assessment for all major public and private sector projects with potential impact on the environment

- progress toward reduction of protection and capital subsidies to large-scale industries and increased allocation of resources to rural industry

- a more active debate on the environmental implications of macroeconomic and sectoral policies during policy formulation, especially among economists and policy makers in the finance, planning, and industry ministries

- progress toward making natural resource pricing and environmental considerations an integral part of the structural and sectoral adjustment negotiations and loans

- increasing use of extended economic analysis of projects, with provisions for internalization and mitigation of environmental effects

Aid organizations may go one step further and monitor actual changes in resource use and the state of the environment through leading resource indicators that should be developed for this purpose (such as rates of deforestation and reforestation, levels of soil erosion and sedimentation, and reduction in biological oxygen demand in water systems) and then attempt to link these changes to the strategy. Of course, the ultimate test of the strategy's success is not the elimination of all symptoms and physical manifestations of environmental degradation but their containment to levels consistent with society's other objectives. In some cases, however, the linkage may be too indirect and tenuous to be meaningful. It is also important to note that in many cases the linkage between the strategy and policy changes must be based on a "before and after" comparison rather than on a "with or without" comparison most appropriate for performance evaluation. The indicator that progress is being made is the lessening and ultimate elimination of the economic manifestations of environmental degradation.

CHAPTER 6

Sustainable Development and Economic Growth

As developing countries struggle to escape poverty and meet the growing aspirations of their still-expanding populations, many perceive the concern for sustainability to be an extra burden added to what is already a Herculean task. If sustainability means that the current generation of poor must endure Spartan conditions so that the next generation will have a better standard of living, it lacks intergenerational justice. If sustainability means, rather, that future generations should be able to enjoy the same standard of living as the current generation, it implies the maintenance of poverty.

Clearly, sustainable development must benefit both current and future generations. It is not simply a matter of temporal trade-offs and intergenerational transfers. It is a matter of cost and efficiency rather than the rate and speed of growth. Sustainability is in fact not attainable without economic growth. Sustainability requires alleviation of poverty, a decline in fertility, the substitution of human capital for natural resources, effective demand for environmental quality, and a responsive supply. These changes cannot take place on a sustainable basis without growth. They are contingent upon the attainment of higher levels of income.

The alarmist prediction that continued economic growth

must lead to ecological disaster or that sustainability will eclipse growth, as well as utopian prescriptions to ban growth and change people's values, derive from a fixation on the physical manifestations and symptoms of environmental degradation: hectares of forest lost, tons of soil eroded, species endangered, tons of pollution generated. The way to attain sustainable growth is to dispense with a preoccupation with the symptoms of environmental degradation and to look for root causes rather than proximate causes.

Why, then, are increasingly scarce resources being used inefficiently and wasted, instead of economized and conserved? The root causes of environmental degradation lie in the dissociation between scarcity and price, benefits and costs, rights and responsibilities, actions and consequences. Too many resources are unowned and unpriced. Others are priced too low, or their depletion is subsidized. Preventing prices from rising in line with growing scarcities and rising social costs distorts the signals that in a well-functioning market would bring about increased efficiency, substitution, conservation, and innovation to restore the balance between supply and demand. The ultimate source of environmental degradation and unsustainability is not growth. It is policy and market failures. To put it simply, you get what you pay for; what you don't pay for, you lose. If a government subsidizes waste, inefficiency, resource depletion, and environmental degradation, that is exactly what it will get. If a population has free and open access to a scarce resource, it will not be a resource for long. Every depleted resource or degraded environment points to a subsidy or a failure to establish the basic conditions that would enable the market to function efficiently. A market failure is nothing but a policy failure, one step removed.

Economic growth generates many benefits: higher standards of living, better education and health, greater longevity, better working conditions, and reduced hours of work. Economic growth also has costs: resource depletion, environmental degradation, ecological disturbance, and widened inequalities, especially during the takeoff stage.

How can the costs of growth be minimized and fully paid for? They must be borne by those who generate them, not by general taxpayers, foreign lenders, or future generations. The principle that the polluter of the environment or beneficiary from natural resources pays is not only fair, but efficient and sustainable as well.

How can polluters and resource users be made to pay the social and developmental costs of their growing wealth? First, governments must eliminate all direct and indirect subsidies, giveaways, and public projects that promote environmental degradation or resource depletion. Second, they should establish the institutions necessary for the emergence and efficient functioning of environmental and resource markets—institutions such as secure, enforceable, and transferable property rights and enforcement of contracts. Third, they must internalize externalities and mitigate any other market failures through a consistent structure of market-based economic incentives and disincentives rather than a patchwork of unenforceable bureaucratic command-and-control regulations. Fourth, they must subject all public projects to rigorous scrutiny, assessment, and valuation of environment effects.

Skeptics ask whether growth is possible if the full environmental costs of growth are paid for. The answer depends on the source of growth. If the growth is derived from appropriating other people's resources or shifting one's own costs onto others, it will not continue. If it is derived from increased efficiency and productivity, it will continue. In fact, empirical studies show that the most important sources of growth are increased efficiency and innovation resulting from accumulated knowledge and expanding human capital.

There is tremendous scope for decoupling economic growth from expanding energy and resource use and advancing environmental degradation. The classic example is Japan, which in 1991 produced twice its output of 1973 with the same amount of energy and significantly reduced emissions. Similarly, industrial growth can be decoupled from toxic waste, urban development from congestion and pollution, agricultural growth from deforestation and soil erosion, and resource extraction from ecological destruction and social dislocation.

The quest for sustainability can be made into a potent force for efficiency, productivity, innovation, and growth, as well as conservation, as some of the cases in this book show—if decision makers do not squander enthusiasm for sustainable development on knee-jerk responses, such as instituting inefficient command-and-control mechanisms. The road to sustainable development passes through an undistorted, competitive, and all-encompassing market that gets the incentives right.

The problem with currently existing markets is that they are neither undistorted nor all-encompassing, particularly in the case of natural resources and the environment. While it is tempting to declare the free market unworkable when it comes to ecology and the environment and to seek to replace it by government fiat, the regrettable experience of the centrally planned economies of Eastern Europe, the threats to state-owned forests throughout the tropical world, and the impotence of command-and-control regulations to contain worldwide environmental degradation dictate otherwise. The best hope is for the state to eliminate the policy-induced distortions of existing markets and to establish the foundations and institutional arrangements necessary for the emergence and efficient functioning of currently absent or thin markets in natural resources and environmental services.

The old argument that natural resources are a gift of nature to be enjoyed freely by all or that the environment is a public good that cannot be traded in markets has been proven faulty by at least three developments. First, natural resources treated as free goods or state property have soon been depleted. The environment as a public good or "everybody's property" has turned out to be "nobody's property." Second, the poor, on whose behalf resources and the environment were ostensibly left outside the domain of the markets, have been the ultimate victims. Third, many innovative approaches, mechanisms, and instruments for bringing natural resources and the environment into the domain of the markets have been developed and successfully tested in recent years.

The role of the state in the struggle for sustainable development is critical and fundamental but is not one of direct management or command and control. The state's role is rather to establish new rules of the game and create an environment that fosters competition, efficiency, and conservation. Only the state can remove the distortions that the state has introduced in the first place. Only the state can establish secure and effective property rights, legal enforcement of contracts, pollution charges and permits, environmental performance bonds, and other institutions, mechanisms, and instruments essential for the emergence and efficient functioning of green markets, on which sustainable development ultimately depends.

APPENDIX A

Tables

TABLE A1

Economic and Financial Analysis of Government-assisted Cattle
Ranches in the Brazilian Amazon

	Net present value (millions of US$)	Total investment outlay (millions of US$)	Return (net present value as % of investment outlay)
Economic analysis			
Base case[a]	−2,824,000	5,143,700	−55
Sensitivity analysis			
Cattle prices assumed doubled	511,380	5,143,700	10
Land prices assumed rising 5% per year more than general inflation rate	−2,300,370	5,143,700	−45
Financial analysis			
Reflecting all investor incentives: tax credits, deductions, and subsidized loans	1,875,400	753,650	249
Sensitivity analysis			
Interest rate subsidies eliminated	849,000	753,650	113
Deductibility of losses against other taxable income eliminated	−658,500	753,650	−87

a. The base case is the projection of the current situation into the future.
SOURCE: Robert Repetto, "Economic Policy Reform for Natural Resource Conservation," Environment Working Paper (Washington, D.C.: World Bank, May 1988).

TABLE A2

Net Social Benefits of Ownership Security in Thailand

| Province | Gross social benefit as percentage of P^a | | Social cost as percent- age of P | Net social benefit as percentage of P | | Mean P (baht per rai) | Net social benefit in baht per rai | |
	For risk- neutral farmer[b]	For risk- averse farmer[b]		For risk- neutral farmer	For risk- averse farmer		For risk- neutral farmer	For risk- averse farmer
Nakhon								
Ratchasim	82.9	38.6	3.3	79.6	35.3	3,448	2,745	1,217
Khon-Kaen	80.5	42.1	3.5	77.0	38.6	3,204	2,467	1,237
Chaiyaphum	41.3	25.3	5.6	35.7	19.7	2,014	719	397
Pooled northeast								
sample	68.2	35.1	4.1	64.1	31.0	2,889	1,852	896

a. P = the price of untitled land. The opportunity cost of capital is assumed to be 12 percent.
b. Risk neutral and risk averse refer to the farmer's attitude toward the risk of being evicted from untitled land.
SOURCE: Gershon Feder, Tongroj Onchan, Yongyuth Chalamwong, and Chira Hongladarom, *Land Policies and Farm Productivity in Thailand* (Baltimore: Johns Hopkins University Press, 1988).

Guidelines for Policies and Projects

In formulating development policies, developing countries may find the following guidelines useful for pursuing the goal of sustainable development:

1. Ensure self-renewal of renewable resources by preventing overexploitation and mismanagement.

2. Prevent unnecessary environmental damage from the extraction and processing of both renewable and nonrenewable resources.

3. Promote recycling where it is economically and environmentally beneficial.

4. Avoid irreversible environmental effects.

5. Undertake environmental protection measures that can be shown to have economic benefits that exceed their economic costs.

6. Emphasize effective protection over rehabilitation on grounds of greater cost-effectiveness.

7. Adopt the principle "users and polluters pay" to internalize scarcity and environmental costs.

8. Assess the environmental effects of sectoral and macroeconomic policies and internalize them, partly by adjust-

ment of these policies and partly by mitigation of residual impacts.

The following are guidelines for designing projects that will help meet the goal of sustainable development:

1. Projects affecting renewable resources should not result in rates of use that exceed the regenerative capacity of these resources or environments. For example, fisheries projects should not lead to overfishing, livestock projects should not lead to overgrazing, irrigation projects should not lead to destruction of watersheds, and agricultural projects should not lead to mining of the soil, excessive soil erosion, and overuse of pesticides.

2. Projects should not lead to irreversible deterioration of the environment. For instance, they should not cause species extinction, habitat destruction, loss of significant biological diversity, or destruction of merit sites (natural and cultural).

3. Projects should not unduly compromise the public's health and safety by, for example, using chemicals such as asbestos, producing hazardous wastes, or building reservoirs in areas of earthquakes or volcanic activity.

4. No projects should displace people or seriously disadvantage certain vulnerable groups, including tribal groups, without mitigatory and compensatory measures that leave them better off.

5. No projects should contravene international environmental agreements (for example, the Montreal Protocol).

6. No projects should significantly modify natural areas designated as national parks, wildlife refuges, biosphere reserves, or World Heritage sites.

7. Planners should minimize unavoidable adverse consequences of projects through site selection, scale adjustment, timing, attenuation, and mitigating measures.

8. Decision makers should balance short-term development gains against long-term environmental degradation or re-

source impairment (trade-offs) or internalize environmental damage through consideration of forgone long-term development benefits. Short-term development often leads to environmental degradation that constrains long-term sustainable development.

9. Projects that involve unnecessary or irreversible damage to the natural resource base and the environment should be avoided.

10. Projects that protect, restore, and enhance the environment and that are based on extended economic appraisal that fully internalize their benefits as well as their costs should be supported. Some examples are reforestation and afforestation; forest and soil conservation; management of rangelands and wildlands; watershed management; fisheries management; protection and management of parks, nature reserves, and wildlife sanctuaries; land titling; irrigation maintenance, rehabilitation, and management; solid waste management; efficient energy pricing; control of urban and industrial pollution; improvement of water quality and sanitation and control of water pollution; prevention of desertification; water supply and sewage improvement; slum upgrading; projects in public health and education; preservation of genetic diversity; integrated pest management; safe disposal of hazardous wastes; coastal zone management; and ecotourism.

11. Decision makers should include environmental effects in the appraisal of all public and large private projects by requiring extended economic analysis that considers a wider set of inputs and outputs than is traditionally considered, extends the relevant space dimension beyond the immediate site of the project to internalize spillover effects, extends the relevant time horizon beyond the useful economic life of the project to internalize long-term effects and residual impacts, and includes indirect effects and intangibles usually left out of cost-benefit analysis. Financial analysis and conventional narrow economic analysis lead to misallocation of resources when significant environmental impacts are involved.

Notes

Chapter 1, "Environmental Degradation: The Magnitude of the Problem"

1. Shifting cultivation is a traditional agricultural practice in which farmers slash and burn forest land, cultivate it for several years, leave it fallow for several years, and then repeat the cycle.

2. See Theodore Panayotou, "Management Concepts for Small-Scale Fisheries: Economic and Social Aspects," FAO Fisheries Technical Paper No. 228 (Rome: Food and Agriculture Organization of the United Nations, 1982).

3. Common property and open-access property are used here interchangeably. Communal property is distinguished from common property by exclusion of other communities and by customary rules of access and management. Unlike common or open-access resources, communal resources are often well-managed (see Case 4 on page 20).

Chapter 2, "Market Failures and Environmental Degradation"

1. Marginal benefit is the incremental benefit derived from the use of an additional unit of an input—for example, the increased rice output from using an additional kilogram of pesticide. Marginal cost is the incremental cost of using an additional unit of input, which is its cost of production plus the damage to other activities or to the environment in general.

2. Joseph Stiglitz, *Economics of the Public Sector* (New York: Norton, 1986), p. 184.

3. The marginal supply cost is the cost of supplying one more unit of the good.

4. Warren C. Baum and Stokes M. Tolbert, *Investing in Development: Lessons from World Bank Experience* (New York: Oxford University Press for the World Bank, 1985), p. 456.

5. Colin W. Clark, "Profit Maximization and the Extinction of Animal Species," *Journal of Political Economy* 81 (August 1973): 950–60.

6. High discount rates cut both ways: they discourage both conservation and exploitation projects that require major investments with future streams of benefits, but on balance conservation is more adversely affected because its benefits are more distant in the future.

7. It must be kept in mind that throughout this book the term "common property" is used as identical to open-access resource. It is to be distinguished from "communal property," which involves well-defined and enforceable community rights over resources.

8. John Krutilla and Anthony Fisher, *The Economics of Natural Environment* (Washington, D.C.: Resources for the Future, 1985).

Chapter 3, "Policy Failures and Environmental Degradation"

1. Here, as in all policy analysis, I assume away the "second-best" problem, that is, the difficulty of knowing whether a policy that does not remove all distortions in the economy is an improvement over the status quo.

2. National Economic and Social Development Board, *The Fifth National Economic and Social Development Plan, 1982–1986* (Bangkok: Office of the Prime Minister, 1982), p. 233.

3. Theodore Panayotou and Somthawin Sungsuwan, "An Econometric Study of the Causes of Tropical Deforestation: The Case of Northeast Thailand," Development Discussion Paper No. 284 (Cambridge, Mass.: Harvard Institute for International Development, 1992).

4. For more details on analytical approaches to be used under various circumstances in the economic analyses of projects, see U.S. Agency for International Development (USAID), *AID Manual for Project Economic Analysis* (Washington, D.C.: USAID, 1987).

5. Peter Rogers, "Fresh Water," in Robert Repetto, ed., *The Global Possible: Resources, Development, and the New Century* (New Haven: Yale University Press, 1985), p. 7.

6. High grading is a tax-induced selective harvesting of the most valuable tree species and sizes and the damage to and waste of the remaining less valuable but still commercially profitable species.

7. The information on deforestation in Honduras comes from the U.S. Agency for International Development.

8. Baum and Tolbert, *Investing in Development*, p. 98.

9. M. S. Khan, "Freshwater Pond Culture in Bangladesh," in Theodore Panayotou, ed., *Small-Scale Fisheries in Asia: Socioeconomic Analysis and Policy* (Ottawa: International Development Research Centre, 1985).

10. Food and Agriculture Organization (FAO)/United Nations Development Program, "Agriculture Mission to Bangladesh," Working Paper 4 (Fisheries Sector) (Rome: FAO, 1977).

11. The information on environmental degradation in Lesotho comes from the U.S. Agency for International Development.

12. Gershon Feder, Tongroj Onchan, Yongyuth Chalamwong, and Chira Hongladarom, *Land Policies and Farm Productivity in Thailand* (Baltimore: Johns Hopkins University Press for the World Bank, 1988).

13. Baum and Tolbert, *Investing in Development*, p. 98.

14. See Feder et al., *Land Policies and Farm Productivity in Thailand.*

15. Progressive land taxation, combined with purchase of land using the land tax revenues and mortgaging of this land to landless farmers, can result in gradual but effective land reform.

16. Thailand Development Research Institute (TDRI), *Thailand Natural Resources Profile* (Bangkok: TDRI, 1987), p. 57.

17. Asian Development Bank (ADB), "Thailand Agricultural Assessment Study" (Manila: ADB, January 1984).

18. *New York Times*, April 16, 1989, p. 1.

19. Ibid.

20. The information about urbanization problems in Santo Domingo comes from the U.S. Agency for International Development.

21. The information on Yemen comes from the U.S. Agency for International Development.

22. "City Lights," *The Economist*, February 18, 1989.

23. For a detailed study of the impact of structural adjustment policies on the environment, see Theodore Panayotou and Chalongphob Sussangkarn, "Structural Adjustment and the Environment: The Case of Thailand," in D. Reed, ed., *Structural Adjustment and the Environment* (Boulder, Colo.: Westview Press, 1992).

Chapter 4, "Achieving Sustainable Development through Policy Reform"

1. Iona Sebastian and Adelaida Alicbusan, "Sustainable Development: Issues in Adjustment Lending Policies," Environment Divisional Paper No. 1989-6 (Washington, D.C.: World Bank, October 1989).

2. Keystone food plants are fruit-producing plants critical to the survival of many animal species in tropical forests.

3. Theodore Panayotou and Peter S. Ashton, *Not by Timber Alone: Economics and Ecology for Sustaining Tropical Forests* (Washington, D.C.: Island Press, 1992).

4. "The Preservation Paradox," *U.S. News and World Report*, April 25, 1988.

5. Also of considerable value is a manual published by the International Union for the Conservation of Nature and Natural Resources entitled "Biological Diversity and Human Economy: Guidelines for Using Economic Incentives to Provide Conservation of Biological Resources."

6. Robert Repetto, *Skimming the Water: Rent-Seeking and the Performance of Public Irrigation Systems* (Washington, D.C.: World Resources Institute, 1986), p. 34.

7. Ibid., p. 33.

8. Lester Ross, *Environmental Policy in China* (Bloomington: Indiana University Press, 1988).

9. Frederick R. Anderson, Allen V. Kneese, Philip D. Reed, Serge Taylor, and Russell B. Stevenson, *Environmental Improvement through Economic Incentives* (Baltimore: Johns Hopkins University Press for Resources for the Future, 1977).

Bibliography

Ahmad, Yusuf J., Salah El Serafy, and Ernst Lutz, eds. *Environmental Accounting for Sustainable Development*. Washington, D.C.: World Bank, 1989.

Anderson, Dennis. *The Economics of Afforestation: A Case Study in Africa*. Baltimore: Johns Hopkins University Press, 1987, p. 68.

Anderson, Frederick R., Allen V. Kneese, Philip D. Reed, Serge Taylor, and Russell B. Stevenson. *Environmental Improvement through Economic Incentives*. Baltimore: Johns Hopkins University Press for Resources for the Future, 1977.

Asian Development Bank (ADB). "Thailand Agricultural Assessment Study." Manila: ADB, January 1984.

Asian Development Bank (ADB) and International Irrigation Management Institute. *Irrigation Service Fees*. Proceedings of the Regional Seminar on Irrigation Service Fees. Manila: ADB, 1986.

Attaviroj, P. "Soil Erosion and Degradation in Northern Thai Upland: An Economic Study." Paper presented at the International Conference on the Economics of Dry Land Degradation and Rehabilitation, Canberra, March 10–14, 1986.

Australian UNESCO Committee for Man and the Biosphere. *Ecological Effects of Increasing Human Activities on Tropical and Sub-Tropical Forest Ecosystems*. Canberra: Australian Government Publishing Services, 1976.

Banerjee, A. K. "A Case of Group Formation in Forest Management." June 1989. Mimeo.

Barber, Edward B. *Economics, Natural Resource Scarcity and Development*. London: Earthscan Publications, 1989.

Baum, Warren C., and Stokes M. Tolbert. *Investing in Development: Lessons from World Bank Experience*. New York: Oxford University Press for the World Bank, 1985.

Binswanger, Hans P. "Brazilian Policies That Encourage Deforestation in the Amazon." Washington, D.C.: World Bank, April 1989.

157

Booth, Anne. *Agricultural Development in Indonesia*. Sydney: ASAA Southeast Asia Publications Series, 1988.

Cernea, Michael M. "User Groups as Producers in Participatory Afforestation Strategies." Development Discussion Paper No. 319. Cambridge, Mass.: Harvard Institute for International Development, 1989.

"City Lights." *The Economist*, February 18, 1989.

Clark, Colin W. "Profit Maximization and the Extinction of Animal Species." *Journal of Political Economy* 81 (August 1973): 950–60.

Clark University Program for International Development. *Renewable Resource Trends in East Africa*. Worcester, Mass.: Clark University, 1984.

Conway, Gordon R., Ibrahim Manwan, and David S. McCauley. *The Sustainability of Agricultural Intensification in Indonesia: A Report of Two Workshops of the Research Group on Agro-Ecosystems*. Jakarta: Ford Foundation and Agency for Agricultural Research and Development, Ministry of Agriculture, Indonesia, December 1984.

Cooter, Robert D. "Inventing Property: Economic Theories of the Origins of Market Property Applied to Papua New Guinea." Berkeley: University of California, 1990. Mimeo.

Davis, Gloria. "Indonesia Forest, Land and Water: Issues in Sustainable Development." Washington, D.C.: World Bank, 1989. Mimeo.

Dhanasetthakarn, Apisak. "More Deforestation since Logging Ban." *The Nation*, June 29, 1989.

Dixon, John A., and Maynard M. Hufschmidt, eds. *Economic Valuation Techniques for the Environment*. Baltimore: Johns Hopkins University Press, 1986.

Dunkerly, Harold B., Alan A. Walters, and John M. Courtney. "Urban Land Policy: Issues and Opportunities." Vol. 2. World Bank Staff Working Paper No. 283. Washington, D.C.: World Bank, 1978.

"The Environment Survey." *The Economist*, September 2, 1989.

Erlanger, Steven. "Indonesia Takes Steps to Protect Rain Forests." *New York Times*, September 26, 1989.

"The Extended Family: A Survey of Indonesia." *The Economist*, August 15, 1987.

Falloux, Francois. "Land Information and Remote Sensing for Renewable Resource Management in Sub-Saharan Africa: A Demand-Driven Approach." Technical Paper No. 108. Washington, D.C.: World Bank, 1989.

Feder, Gershon, Tongroj Onchan, Yongyuth Chalamwong, and Chira Hongladarom. *Land Policies and Farm Productivity in Thailand*. Baltimore: Johns Hopkins University Press for the World Bank, 1988.

Food and Agriculture Organization (FAO). *Integrated Pest Management in Rice in Indonesia*. Jakarta: FAO, May 1988.

Food and Agriculture Organization (FAO)/United Nations Development Program. "Agriculture Mission to Bangladesh." Working Paper 4 (Fisheries Sector). Rome: FAO, 1977.

Gillis, Malcolm. "West Africa: Resource Management Policies and the Tropical Forest." In Robert Repetto and Malcolm Gillis, eds., *Public Policies and the Misuse of Forest Resources*. New York: Cambridge University Press, 1988.

Goodland, Robert, and George Ledec. "Environmental Management in Sustainable Economic Development." *International Association of Impact Assessment* (Spring 1987).

Gorse, Jean Eugene, and David R. Steeds. *Desertification in the Sahelian and Sudanian Zones of West Africa*. Technical Paper No. 61. Washington, D.C.: World Bank, 1987.

"Government to Abolish Subsidy for Utilization of Pesticide." *The Jakarta Post*, December 2, 1988.

Johnson, Sam H., III. *Physical and Economic Impacts of Sedimentation on Fishing Activities: Nam Pong, Northeast Thailand*. Urbana-Champaign: University of Illinois, 1984.

Khan, M. S. "Freshwater Pond Culture in Bangladesh." In Theodore Panayotou, ed., *Small-Scale Fisheries in Asia: Socioeconomic Analysis and Policy*. Ottawa: International Development Research Centre, 1985.

Krutilla, John, and Anthony Fisher. *The Economics of Natural Environment*. Washington, D.C.: Resources for the Future, 1985.

Ledec, George, and Robert Goodland. *Wildlands: Their Protection and Management in Economic Development*. Washington, D.C.: World Bank, 1988.

Leonard, H. Jeffrey. *Natural Resources and Economic Development in Central America*. New Brunswick, N.J.: Transaction Books, 1987.

Mahar, Dennis J. *Government Policies and Deforestation in Brazil's Amazon Region*. Washington, D.C.: World Bank, 1989.

McCoy-Thompson, Meri. "Sliding Slopes Break Thai Logjam." *World Watch*, September/October 1989.

McNeely, Jeffrey A. *Economics and Biological Diversity: Developing and Using Economic Incentives to Conserve Biological Resources*. Gland, Switzerland: International Union for Conservation of Nature and Natural Resources, 1988.

_____. "How Dams and Wildlife Can Coexist: Natural Habitats, Agriculture, and Major Water Resource Development Projects in Tropical Asia." *Journal of Conservation Biology* 1, no. 3 (October 3, 1987).

_____. "Protected Areas and Human Ecology: How National Parks Can Contribute to Sustaining Societies of the Twenty-first Century." In David Western and Mary C. Pearl, eds., *Conservation for the Twenty-first Century*. Oxford: Oxford University Press, 1989.

Mirante, Edith. "A 'Teak War' Breaks Out in Burma." *Earth Island Journal* (Summer 1989).

National Economic and Social Development Board. *The Fifth National Economic and Social Development Plan, 1982–1986*. Bangkok: Office of the Prime Minister, 1982.

National Research Council Panel on Common Property Resource Management/Board on Science and Technology for International Development Office of International Affairs. *Proceedings of the Conference on Common Property Resource Management*. Washington, D.C.: National Academy Press, 1986.

Panayotou, Theodore. "Economics, Environment and Development." Development Discussion Paper No. 259. Cambridge, Mass.: Harvard Institute for International Development, 1987.

_____. "The Economics of Man-Made Natural Disasters: The Case of the 1988 Landslides in South Thailand." In National Operations Center (NOC), National Economic and Social Development Board (NESDB), and U.S. Agency for International Development (USAID), *Safeguarding the Future: Restoration and Sustainable Development in the South of Thailand.* Bangkok: NOC/NESDB/USAID, August 1989.

_____. "Management Concepts for Small-Scale Fisheries: Economic and Social Aspects." Food and Agriculture Organization (FAO) Fisheries Technical Paper No. 228. Rome: FAO, 1982.

_____. "Natural Resources and the Environment in the Economies of Asia and the Near East: Growth, Structural Change and Policy Reform." Cambridge, Mass.: Harvard Institute for International Development, July 1989. Mimeo.

_____. "Natural Resource Management: Strategies for Sustainable Asian Agriculture in the 1990's." Development Discussion Paper. Cambridge, Mass.: Harvard Institute for International Development, September 1988.

_____. "Thailand's Management of Natural Resources for Sustainable Development: Market Failures, Policy Distortions and Policy Options." Cambridge, Mass.: Harvard Institute for International Development, May 1988. Mimeo.

Panayotou, Theodore, and Peter S. Ashton. *Not by Timber Alone: Economics and Ecology for Sustaining Tropical Forests.* Washington, D.C.: Island Press, 1992.

Panayotou, Theodore, and Somthawin Sungsuwan. "An Econometric Study of the Causes of Tropical Deforestation: The Case of Northeast Thailand." Development Discussion Paper No. 284. Cambridge, Mass.: Harvard Institute for International Development, 1992.

Panayotou, Theodore, and Chalongphob Sussangkarn. "Structural Adjustment and the Environment: The Case of Thailand." In D. Reed, ed., *Structural Adjustment and the Environment.* Boulder, Colo.: Westview Press, 1992.

Peters, C. M., A. H. Gentry, and R. Mendelsohn. "Valuation of a Tropical Forest in Peruvian Amazonia." *Nature* 339 (1989): 655–56.

Pezzey, John. "Economic Analysis of Sustainable Growth and Sustainable Development." Environment Department Working Paper No. 15. Washington, D.C.: World Bank, March 1989.

Program for International Development, Clark University, in cooperation with National Environment Secretariat, Ministry of Environment and Natural Resources, Government of Kenya. *Resources, Management Population and Local Institutions in Katheka: A Case Study of Effective Natural Resources Management in Machakos, Kenya.* Worcester, Mass.: Clark University, 1988.

Reed, D., ed. *Structural Adjustment and the Environment.* Boulder, Colo.: Westview Press, 1992.

Repetto, Robert. "Economic Policy Reform for Natural Resource Conservation." Environment Working Paper. Washington, D.C.: World Bank, May 1988.

_____. *The Forest for the Trees? Government Policies and the Misuse of Forest Resources.* Washington, D.C.: World Resources Institute, 1988.

_____. *Skimming the Water: Rent-Seeking and the Performance of Public Irrigation Systems.* Washington, D.C.: World Resources Institute, 1986.

Rogers, Peter. "Fresh Water." In Robert Repetto, ed., *The Global Possible: Resources, Development, and the New Century.* New Haven: Yale University Press, 1985.

Ross, Lester. *Environmental Policy in China.* Bloomington: Indiana University Press, 1988.

Schramm, Gunter, and Jeremy J. Warford, eds. *Environmental Management and Economic Development.* Baltimore: Johns Hopkins University Press, 1989.

Sebastian, Iona, and Adelaida Alicbusan. "Sustainable Development: Issues in Adjustment Lending Policies." Environment Divisional Paper No. 1989-6. Washington, D.C.: World Bank, October 1989.

Southgate, David, and David Pearce. "Agricultural Colonization and Environmental Degradation in Frontier Developing Economies." Washington, D.C.: World Bank, October 1988. Mimeo.

Spears, John. "Containing Tropical Deforestation: A Review of Priority Areas for Technological and Policy Research." Environment Department Working Paper No. 10. Washington, D.C.: World Bank, October 1988.

Spears, John, and Edward S. Ayensu. "Resources, Development and the New Century: Forestry." In Robert Repetto, ed., *The Global Possible: Resources, Development and the New Century.* New Haven: Yale University Press, 1985.

Srivardhana, Ruandoj. *The Nam Pong Case Study: Some Lessons to Be Learned.* Honolulu: Environment and Policy Institute, East-West Center, 1982.

Stiglitz, Joseph. *Economics of the Public Sector.* New York: Norton, 1986.

Szulc, Tad. "Brazil's Amazonian Frontier." In Andrew Maguire and Janet Welsh Brown, eds., *Bordering on Trouble: Resources and Politics in Latin America.* Bethesda, Md.: Adler & Adler, 1986.

Thailand Development Research Institute (TDRI). *Thailand Natural Resources Profile.* Bangkok: TDRI, 1987.

Thomas, Vinod. "Pollution Control in São Paulo, Brazil: Costs, Benefits, and Effects on Industrial Location." World Bank Staff Working Paper No. 501. Washington, D.C.: World Bank, 1981.

"Traffic Jams: The City, the Commuter and the Car." *The Economist,* February 18, 1989.

U.S. Agency for International Development (USAID). *AID Manual for Project Economic Analysis.* Washington, D.C.: USAID, 1987.

_____. *Development and the National Interest: U.S. Economic Assistance into the 21st Century.* Washington, D.C.: USAID, 1989.

_____. *Environmental and Natural Resource Management in Central America: A Strategy for AID Assistance.* Washington, D.C.: USAID, 1988.

_____. *Environmental and Natural Resource Management in the Asia and Near East Region: Strategies for AID in the 1990's.* Washington, D.C.: USAID, 1989.

_____. "Safeguarding the Future: Restoration and Sustainable Development in the South of Thailand." USAID Team Report. Bangkok: USAID, 1989.

Watson, Peter L., and Edward P. Holland. "Relieving Traffic Congestion: The Singapore Area License Scheme." World Bank Staff Working Paper No. 281. Washington, D.C.: World Bank, June 1978.

"Win Some, Lose Some." *Far Eastern Economic Review*, October 27, 1988.

World Commission on Environment and Development. *Our Common Future*. New York: Oxford University Press, 1987.

World Resources Institute and International Institute for Environment and Development. *World Resources 1986*. New York: Basic Books, 1986.

_____. *World Resources 1987*. New York: Basic Books, 1987.

_____. *World Resources 1988–1989*. New York: Basic Books, 1988.

World Resources Institute, World Bank, and United Nations Development Programme. *Tropical Forests: A Call for Action*. Vols. 1 and 2. Washington, D.C.: World Resources Institute, October 1985.

Index

Agricultural sector
demand for forest land by,
79–80
effect of industrial promotion
on, 94
extensification and
intensification in, 4–5
policy reform in, 100–101
with reduction in input
subsidies, 101–3
as source of pollution, 87–88
Aid agencies. *See* Development
assistance agencies
Air pollution
emission charges for, 131
in industrialized urban areas,
83–85
Asian Development Bank (ADB),
113nn1,3,4

Baum, Warren C., 47, 79
Benefits
discounting of future, 50–52
of positive externalities, 40
when transaction costs exceed,
43–44
See also Marginal benefit
Biological diversity
as global public good, 46
policies to conserve, 121–25
value of, 4, 23
Buffer zones, 123–24

Capital market liberalization, 96
Charges. *See* Effluent charges;
Emission charges; User
charges
Clark, Colin, 50
Collective action, 119
Commodities
resource-based and tradable, 96
unpriced or low-priced natural
resource, 37–39

valuation of non-marketplace,
124
Common property. *See*
Open-access resources
Communal property, 37, 153n1.3
See also Buffer zones
Communal resource
management, 13, 16–17,
18–19, 20–21, 118–19, 153n1.3
Competition
insufficient, 48–50
role of, 33
Congestion, urban
charges as method to reduce,
131
policy in Singapore for, 92–93
policy responses to, 89–90
Conservation
benefits of, in developing
countries, 124–25
conditions for forest, 121
estimating willingness to pay
for, 124
incentives for, 125
lack of mechanism for, 126–27
uncertainty about benefits of, 54
of wildlands in Indonesia, 28–29
See also Nonuse value (in
conservation); Use value (in
conservation); Valuation
Costs
exceeding benefits, 43–44
external, 39, 40–41
of information, 42
internalization of
environmental, 7
related to rationing, 90
See also Benefits; Externalities;
Social costs
Credit
high cost of, 50–52
informal, 50, 51
lack of access to, 80, 96

ICEG Academic Advisory Board